Forgiveness is Healing

Forgiveness is Healing

RUSS PARKER

Foreword by Bishop Morris Maddocks

DARTON · LONGMAN + TODD

First published in 1993 by
Darton, Longman and Todd Ltd (Daybreak imprint)
1 Spencer Court
140–142 Wandsworth High Street
London SW18 4JJ

Reprinted 1996, 1997, 1999, 2001 and 2004 (Darton Longman and Todd imprint)

ISBN 0–232–51960–9

A catalogue record for this book is available
from the British Library

Cover design by Leigh Hurlock

Phototypeset by Intype London Ltd
Printed and bound in Great Britain
by CPI Bath

This book is dedicated
to the memory of my mum,
Connie Parker, née Bleach
(1921–1992)
without whom I would have nothing to say.
I will always love her
and be grateful for her love of me.

Contents

Foreword

Confronted by the world scene today, it would be hard to deny that one of the greatest needs for the contemporary human race is forgiveness. A Christian might well add that the redemptive work of Christ on the cross, through which forgiveness is made effective, is the ultimate solution and the only remedy profound enough to meet that need. Russ Parker's book on forgiveness could hardly be more timely.

Forgiveness is a subject whose depths are hard to plumb, but the writer here opens up many of its implications. The matter of personal forgiveness is enlightened by examples from his own ministry which has been rich and varied. But he also treats of the corporate need for forgiveness and in the appendices he offers some practical ways of doing this in the context of worship.

A helpful chapter on the healing of memories is followed by some guidelines on the deliverance ministry and in both the writer stresses the vital part played by forgiveness. I also found that I resonated with the final chapter on healing the land through forgiveness.

Forgiveness is a costly business and I am grateful that Russ Parker does not blur any edges nor pull any punches. 'Forgiveness is confrontational' he states. It is not easy 'even with the help of God's grace', because it always exposes and challenges, rendering us vulnerable. This is a book that does not seek to 'heal the wounds of my people lightly', for the author is not afraid to face the fact of sin.

I value Russ as a colleague on my staff for his deep ministry to people. I am sure that this book will be of like value to

many and I pray that the Lord will mightily use it for the
extension of his kingdom and the healing of his people.

Bishop Morris Maddocks
Co-founder of the Acorn Christian Healing Trust

Acknowledgements

Thanks are due to the following for permission to quote copyright material: Cairns Publications, from *Prayer at Night* by the Revd James E. Cotter; Paulist Press, from *Healing Life's Hurts* by Matthew and Dennis Linn; SPCK, from *Power Lines* by David Adam; Thankyou Music, from *Lord Have Mercy on Us* by Graham Kendrick and *I Get So Excited, Lord* by Mick Ray.

Introduction

On Sunday 17 September 1978 a handshake between two former adversaries was watched by millions of people on television. Abba Eban, an Israeli diplomat and United Nations representative, said that it was 'one of the great land marks in mediation'. The two men in question were Anwar Sadat, the President of Egypt, and Menachem Begin, President of Israel. The event took place in the living room of former President Jimmy Carter's summer retreat of Camp David. It was, in effect, the first ever peace treaty to be agreed upon between Israel and another Arab nation. Within six months the treaty was formally signed in Washington DC and Israel began withdrawing her troops from occupied Sinai. Each country opened its borders to the other and the routines of normal living very slowly began to replace the ravages of decades of open hostility.

The watching world could hardly believe it was happening and a wave of optimism for bringing peace to the Middle East began to circulate within the major nations of the world. However, forgiveness and peace have never been a cheaply won prize. Very often the offer of restoration has stirred up the very bitterness it has sought to cure. Forgiveness can bring both risk and relief, openness or opposition to the one who offers it as well as to the one who receives it. Therefore it was no surprise, though very sad, that some time afterwards President Sadat was assassinated as he was reviewing a military parade. Apparently the perpetrators belonged to a particular party of Islamic fundamentalists who objected to his fraternization with the 'enemy' state of Israel. One man's freedom became another's political poison.

This should come as no surprise to us, as it was the generous

and liberal way in which Jesus forgave sinners that so incensed
and aroused the opposition of some scribes and Pharisees.
David Runcorn points out that in any case real forgiveness will
always carry with it a sense of scandal.[1] It is as if there is a voice
inside each person which wants to cry out, 'Just a moment, you
can't do that! That is taking forgiveness too far.' This was
surely the reaction of the elders who stared in unbelief and
bitterness as Jesus refused to condemn the woman found in
adultery and simply encouraged her to go and live a better life
(John 8:1–11). His acts of forgiveness brought relief to the man
lowered through the hole in the roof as well as to the prostitute
who anointed his feet with ointment. No doubt for the young
man on the stretcher, being forgiven both removed an internal
moral blockage to his life and also released faith in him to
believe in God for his physical healing. For the sinful woman
who interrupted Jesus in the Pharisee's house, her forgiveness
meant that she was restored to her rightful place in the community and she went out of the house in love with God and
determined to live a new life. However, such healing also
brought with it the risk of rejection from those who disapproved
of his actions (Mark 2:5–7; Luke 7:49). They not only questioned his right to offer forgiveness but refused to see its bene-
fits in others, becoming blind therefore to the potential for
healing, and at the same time they began to devise ways of
silencing him. Forgiveness has this two-edged response about
it, it can bring healing to one and hostility from another.

By definition, therefore, forgiveness is confrontational. It
exposes and challenges the 'be-attitudes' of both the forgiver
and the forgiven. It uncovers what is going on in both the giver
and receiver when forgiveness is on offer. We must not imagine
that it is easy for us to forgive even with the help of God's
grace. This is often because in the very act of forgiving we must
also let go of our hurt or sense of outrage at what the other has
done to us. To forgive another is to enter into a commitment to
love them. Jesus coupled the themes of loving and forgiving
enemies in the same sermon given on the Mount (Matthew
5:43–44; 6:14–15). Forgiving another often confronts our own

inner hurt which we may not yet be prepared to yield for healing.

This is well illustrated in the experience of the former Dutch evangelist and Bible teacher, Corrie Ten Boom, whose exploits of faith have been made into a popular film called *The Hiding Place*. During the Nazi occupation of her country she and her sister, along with other members of her family, hid a number of Dutch Jews in their home. Eventually they were betrayed and sent to a German concentration camp where they suffered many hardships, one of which was the death of Corrie's sister. When liberation came she was set free from the camp, but her hate and hurt took a lot longer to heal and free. Yet she eventually set out on the journey of forgiveness and in time was preaching forgiveness all over the world and especially to the German people. In forgiving she believed she had discovered the only power that could heal the history of hate for the people of Europe.

After she had preached her message of reconciliation in a church in Munich one Sunday, she was approached by a man who had formerly been a prison guard at the concentration camp. He held out his hand to her and apparently at the same time expressed his joy and relief that he could be forgiven by her, especially as he too was now a Christian. Corrie froze at his friendly approach and all the bitterness and memories of his cruelties flooded into her mind. She could not forgive him. He was happy at the prospect of receiving her fellowship but she was in pain at the thought of giving it. She struggled with her feelings as she was confronted with her unwillingness to forgive him, as well as her unhealed hurt. She prayed, 'Jesus, I can't forgive this man. Forgive me.' Immediately she felt forgiven for not forgiving and this freed her to take the former guard's hand and free him from his terrible past and also free herself from hers.[2]

Neither must we imagine that receiving forgiveness is necessarily the easy relief that we anticipate. To be forgiven is to see how our actions have both outraged and called for a demonstration of love to heal the effects of the damage we have caused. It can be a very uncomfortable place to be because it means we are to own up to our actions and allow ourselves to be weak enough to be loved and forgiven. This is so ably expressed in the following poem by Jim Cotter:

When we receive the forgiveness of another,
the depths of our personalities are disturbed.
For it means that the worst in us has been accepted –
and that means a kind of death.
We have no need to fight our own worst selves any more.
And it is hard to receive this truth.
We turn against our forgiver in self-justification.
How dare you accept me as I am and not condemn me?
So folk turn against Christ for accepting them.
But God's forgiveness is without condition.
It sweeps us off our feet.
We want to make conditions,
so that there can still be a core under our control.
Let go completely –
this is death –
but it is necessary if we are to find life.
To let go into God.[3]

It is the struggle we have actually to experience forgiveness that often indicates its power to heal. For some years now I have been the Director of a Christian Counselling Centre in the village of Ibstock in Leicestershire. We have a team of twenty trained counsellors and have referrals from both churches and secular caring agencies. So often we have found that at the heart of much pain and illness is the refusal to forgive or to be forgiven. Yet once the door to forgiving has been opened the results can be quite remarkable. I remember working with one person who had been struggling with a history of sexual abuse committed by her father when she was only six years old. She had a deep self-loathing, as well as a lot of repressed anger towards her father which she had never voiced. During one of the counselling sessions she poured out the anger she had never allowed to be heard. It was as if the little girl who had been locked up inside herself had been freed to tell her story. The anger was quite appropriate and it took the form of telling her father (as if he was present with us in the room) that he had no right to do what he did. Then once the hurt and anger had been given a voice, she forgave her father and let go of holding on to the bitterness which she had nursed against him for over thirty years. The result of this experience was that she literally 'came back to life'. The lethargy and lack of energy, characteristic of her life, simply disappeared and she rediscovered her capacity for joy and warmth. Her husband reported that he had a new marriage and all plans for divorce, the original reason for coming for counsel, were cancelled.

Other similar occasions have included a father who let go of his grievance against God for the premature death of his son and suddenly found his faith returned and he came back to being an active member of his church; a pensioner who was healed of long-term back pain when she received forgiveness for giving away an unwanted daughter for adoption; a church minister who reported noticeable growth and renewal in his church when he asked God to forgive him and others who had wrongly ministered there down the years. In all of these circumstances the experience of forgiveness had been the key to unlocking the damage caused in the past, releasing sin and hurt and bringing the healing presence of Jesus to the needs concerned. To be forgiven provides us with so much potential and power for healing in a variety of ways. It is no small wonder therefore that when John records some of the last acts and teachings of Jesus before his ascension he includes the reference to receiving the Holy Spirit for, amongst other ministries, setting people free through forgiveness (John 20:21-3). We have been called and given this mighty resource for the healing of people and nations, but it comes with great risk and cost. It is these healing consequences of forgiveness, along with their possible hostile responses, which form the main focus of this book.

HEALING HARVEST[4]

O memory of a painful time,
Are you seed or stone?

A dark and deadly tomb,
Or seed with life to bloom?
Only if I say 'I want you',
Will I really know.

O sprouting seed, are you angry
At the dark and choking dirt?
What grates your tender shoot
And blocks your chosen route?
Only if I say 'I forgive you',
Will I really know.

O tender shoot, are you bargaining,
Demanding sun before you grow?
Or would you rather as the sun
Pour warm love on everyone?
Only if I say 'I forgive you first',
Will I really know.

O roots, do you wander depressed
Searching in drought for tears?
Or do you need more sun
To dry the tears that run?
Only if I say 'Forgive me',
Will I really know.

O golden wheat, can you accept
The gifts of pulsing seed?
Are you wheat or golden bread?
Are you bread of Christ instead?
Only if I say 'Thank you',
Will I really know.

Unless a grain of wheat
Falls into the earth and dies.
It remains alone
But if it dies,
It bears much fruit.

1

Forgiveness in Action

*I learned about forgiveness, not by reading good books,
but by listening to good forgivers.*

Lewis Smedes[1]

JESUS THE MODEL FORGIVER

When Jesus formally mapped out his calling and ministry he
declared himself to be a forgiver. Luke records this dramatic
moment as following on from two encounters with the power
of the Holy Spirit. The first was his baptism in the Jordan when
he was filled with the Spirit (Luke 4:1), and the second was his
battling with temptation in the wilderness from which he
returned in the power of the Spirit (Luke 4:14). Now comes
the occasion when he enters the synagogue at Nazareth to
preach and proclaim for the first time. He reads from the sixty-
first chapter of the prophet Isaiah:

> The Spirit of the Sovereign Lord is on me,
> because he has anointed me
> to preach good news to the poor.
> He has sent me to proclaim freedom for the prisoners
> and recovery of sight for the blind,
> to release the oppressed,
> to proclaim the year of the Lord's favour. (Luke 4:18–19)

It is interesting to note that the same Greek word (*aphesis*) is
used for both freedom and release, and that it is one of the
standard words for forgiveness in the New Testament. This fits
in very well with the Hebrew words used in the original version

which denote being opened or lightened, and liberty. To give the full impact of this, we could legitimately translate the passages as follows:

> He has sent me to proclaim forgiveness to the prisoners
> and recovery of sight to the blind,
> to forgive the oppressed,
> to proclaim the year of the Lord's favour. (Luke 4:18–19)

Straight away this broadens out the impact of forgiveness to include the healing not only of our sins but of the effects of such sins upon ourselves and those whom we may have damaged. This is why James Emerson was at pains to stress that forgiveness was not so much an exercise of balancing the books of a ledger, in which God's forgiveness balanced out the weight of our sins, but an experience through which we were freed into a new life of growth. He called this 'realized forgiveness'.[2] Such freedom gives us the healing we need to see our lives with more objectivity and insight and then, by the grace of God, the power to choose more creatively a way forward for ourselves. Surely this is what the Apostle Paul meant when he talked about the Christian being a new creature in Christ Jesus (2 Corinthians 5:17f). The writer of the Letter to Barnabas expressed it well when he wrote, 'Since then he has renewed us by the forgiveness of sin, he made us another product, and we have the soul of children as though he were creating us again.'[3]

Bultmann says that because this forgiveness of Jesus is linked to the prophecy of John the Baptist (Luke 1:77), who was to prepare the way for the Messiah, it is actually an eschatological blessing and therefore brings total renewal.[4] He means that forgiveness not only releases us for the now but points the way forward to a life to be lived through the last days and on into eternity. This only confirms what we have established so far, namely that forgiveness is within the gift of Jesus and is a work made possible by the anointing power of the Holy Spirit. We can see that Jesus continuously focused upon the need to forgive throughout his ministry culminating in some of his last words from the cross, 'Father, forgive them, for they do not know what they are doing' (Luke 23:34). Whilst we cannot assume from this prayer that ignorance is a basis for forgiveness, nevertheless, so mighty was its effects that it is more than likely, according to some commentators like Wiersbe and Geldenhuys, that it postponed God's judgement on the nation for almost forty years and so gave additional opportunities to be saved (cf. Acts 3:17–19).[5] Interestingly enough, the very next thing that Jesus does, as recorded by Luke, is to promise one of the thieves that he would be forgiven enough to share Paradise with him that day.

We have already noted the almost flamboyant and ready way in which Jesus forgave people. What is even more remarkable is that in the two specific cases mentioned of Jesus forgiving individuals, there is not one word spoken by the person in need. In the case of the man lowered down by his four friends, the sick man is silent and motionless; Jesus, though, is not only aware of the faith of his friends, because he looks at what is in their faces (Mark 2:5), he is also in touch with what is going on inside the paralytic man and decides that his first and perhaps most important need is forgiveness. Even after he is healed he is silent, perhaps shocked to be standing up and free from his guilt. The sinful woman who interrupts the theological debate amongst the men in Simon the Pharisee's house is much more mobile but equally non-verbal. She cries and lets her tears fall on Jesus' feet, and then proceeds to mop up the tears with her hair (Luke 7:38). No doubt there was shock amongst them all at the way in which Jesus was happy to be touched by the woman, but their level of tolerance may well have been shattered when she produced the jar of ointment and anointed Jesus' feet with it. It is quite likely that the ointment was used formerly to attract her many customers; now she was using it on Jesus.

Reading this account we are allowed to know what Simon himself was thinking about Jesus when all this was happening: 'If this man were a prophet, he would know who is touching him and what kind of woman she is – that she is a sinner' (Luke 7:39). There follows an interesting and provocative comparison which Jesus makes between the lack of a traditional greeting and hospitality from Simon and the fulsome way in which the woman had greeted him. It begins rather humorously and yet quite to the point with Jesus asking Simon, 'Do you see this woman?' (Luke 7:44). Of course he did, he had been doing nothing else ever since she had come into his house! Yet the tragic reality was that Simon, although looking at all her actions, had only seen the sinful woman of his judgementalism and not the repenting woman whom Jesus welcomed. In fact he had not seen the woman at all. The point is eloquently made: it is the forgiving heart which is open to and aware of the healing needed in another. An unforgiving heart is not only blind to the needs of others but is also blind to its own need of healing.

Jesus not only modelled the life of a forgiver by his actions but also by his teaching. In both of the cases mentioned above he was caught up in the controversy of his authority and free-dom to forgive. However, he used both occasions to underline the fact that he does have the mandate and the power to forgive. This is important because it is on the basis of this authority to forgive that he commands us to go and do likewise. Jesus is the first forgiver and because our lives are lived 'in him' we too can become forgivers. Emil Brunner said that it was precisely this factor which was the really new element in Jesus' style of teaching; he did not present forgiveness as a general truth, but his teaching was to provoke us to experience and be granted forgiveness as a fact for ourselves and to pass on to others.[6] An obvious example of applying the reality of the first forgiver is that of healing past hurts where progress is made when we can first call upon Jesus to forgive the one who has offended and hurt us, and his work energizes us to forgive in the power of his forgiveness. Let me give an example of what I mean by this.

Some years ago I was asked to do some work with someone who had been battling with the implications of a disturbing dream which she had been having for almost forty years. The focus of the dream was that of a little girl in a dishevelled dress sitting on the knees of a man whose face she could not make out clearly enough to recognize. The dream picture actually reflected the known facts that she had been sexually assaulted by an uncle for some time beginning when she was about six years old. The fact that his face was obscured in the dream spoke about her reluctance to confront or come to terms with the fact that a relative whom she loved had been responsible. The turning point in her counselling came when, using her dream picture as a focus for faith and action, she invited Jesus to step into her personal reality and bring his healing to her, so that the dream and the past it continuously reflected would no longer have power over her. She was quite surprised when she saw, in her extended dream work, that Jesus, far from rebuking the uncle in question, actually forgave him. She felt that if Jesus could forgive then so could she! His work of forgiveness enabled her to do hers. It was only after she had forgiven him that she could voice her feelings of disgust and anger which had been bottled up inside for many years. Her work of forgiving released her hurt feelings which she could then hand over to God for healing. I am happy to report that subsequently she was able to redirect her life and marriage which were in danger of collapsing.

Not only does Jesus establish by his teaching that he is the first forgiver, but he also leaves us with no doubts that we are to practise forgiveness as a norm in our lives or suffer the consequences of stunted growth. He presents this most graphically in the parable of the prodigal son, which could equally be called the parable of the forgiving father or the parable of the unforgiving brother (Luke 15:11–32). Whichever title we prefer, there is no mistaking the fact that the story is told to illustrate the creative power of forgiveness and the destructive power of unforgiveness. The wayward son has greedily spent his inheritance and has now come to the end of his road. He is friendless and reduced to feeding pigs for a living. Then he has a moment of awareness and repentance. He rightly confesses that he has sinned against his father and against heaven. It is interesting to notice how Jesus in telling this story underlines that our sins against one another also constitute a sin against God. The son thereby concludes that he is no longer worthy to be called a son and wishes to be taken back as a hired servant (15:19). However, the father's forgiveness does not constitute a demotion to servanthood but a celebration to live a new life. The son repeats his confession but is grandly and rudely interrupted with an embrace and an exhortation to enjoy a renewed life. The elder brother, though, sees such free and full forgiveness as a waste of love and patience. He is quite convinced that the prodigal will have to earn his way back into the family. Doubtless he would have been quite happy to see his younger brother installed in the servants' quarters. It is sad and ironic that the older brother obviously believed that his own right to his father's love and celebration depended upon his capacity to work productively. When the father says, 'Everything I have is yours' (15:31), there is one thing surely not included, and that is the father's heart to forgive and receive back a son who had virtually been given up for dead.

In telling this story Jesus also offers us a moment of reflection to become aware of where we stand on the issue of offering forgiveness. Do we celebrate with the father or criticize like the older brother? Perhaps another reason for telling this story is to illustrate the sheer impossibility of our being able to forgive without the presence of Christ in our lives. 'Forgiveness is an exotic, which Christ brought with him from heaven.'[7] Our natural inclination, if we are honest, is to be like that hard-working brother who feels he has been overlooked or cheated by the easy healing and restoration given to his brother who seems to have had his cake and eaten it. This also says something about our indignation sometimes being disguised jealousy because someone else has done something we would like to do! We must not fool ourselves into thinking that forgiving another is an easy option or a work to be carried out in a moment, once for all. I can well imagine the gasp in Peter's voice when in answer to his question about how many times must he forgive his brother, Jesus replied, 'seventy times seven' (Matthew 18:21–2). C. S. Lewis said that the meaning of Jesus' reply was not that he had set a limit on how many times you can forgive another for his or her various sins against you, but an indication that every time the same sin came to mind you forgave that person again and again. This was to be continued until the pain of the offence and the memory of the moment diminished so much as to be of no further account. Truly, forgiveness can be said to be love's toughest work and greatest risk.[8]

Jesus went on to reinforce the necessity and power of forgiveness by linking effective forgiving with personal release and growth (Matthew 6:12ff), productive praying (Mark 11:24–5) and fruitful fellowship (Matthew 5:23, cf. 2 Corinthians 2:6–7). We shall therefore examine in later chapters just how forgiveness affects such different dimensions of healing and growth. Let us take, then, from the model of Jesus the necessity to forgive and our utter need of his personal presence and power in our lives if we too are going to be model forgivers. Let us now go on to answer the question about what it is that lies at the very heart of the action in forgiveness which enables it to be such a healing tool.

THE ACTION IN FORGIVENESS

This dynamic action of forgiveness is further revealed when we look at the seven basic words used in the Bible to translate our one word forgive. According to Emerson, the Hebrew word most often used for forgiveness in the Old Testament is *nasa* which means 'to have a weight lifted away'.[9] Its Greek equivalent, both for the New Testament and for the Septuagint Bible, is *aphiemi* which basically means 'let go' or 'send away'. Apparently the deaf and dumb sign language for forgiveness is signed by wiping the palm of one hand firmly across the other as if removing any stain or mess that clings to it.[10] This picture of forgiveness as a wiping away of offences is confirmed by Paul's words in Colossians which couple the forgiveness of sins with the idea of 'cancelling' the unfavourable record of our debts (Colossians 2:13–14). The word here is *exaleipho* and occurs five times in the New Testament; on each occasion its basic action is that of wiping out or away. In classical usage it is used to describe a range of things such as the whitewashing of a wall, anointing with oil and striking a name off a roll. Jim

Graham says that its basic imagery is that of obliterating something as you would chalk writing on a slate.[11]

In this way our sins are wiped out and the record of condemnation is written off. 'Repent then, and turn to God, so that
your sins may be wiped out (AV = blotted out), that times
of refreshing may come from the Lord' (Acts 3:19). What a
marvellous picture we can begin to construct then of God
letting go of the many sins he could legitimately hold against
us as he chooses rather to forgive. This same word is also used
to translate the Hebrew words *kaphar*, which means 'to cover'
or 'make atonement' (also translated as 'to wipe clean the
face',[12] and *salach* which means 'to let go' or 'to lift up', according to Gesenius.[13] The remaining three words basically convey
variations on the same theme of letting go or lifting away.[14]

At the heart of the action of forgiveness, therefore, is the
decision to let go. This is an action principally carried out by
God and, because of this, by those who would live by his name
and power. I was forcefully reminded of the dynamic nature
of letting go many years ago when I read the Jungle Doctor
stories written for children by Dr John White. Amongst them
there was the graphic tale of how to catch a monkey. You
begin the operation by taking a coconut and chopping off the
end of it. The nut is hollowed out and then filled with ground
nuts which the monkey will easily detect owing to its developed
sense of smell. The coconut is then fixed to a tree so that it
cannot be removed. Finally, the would-be captors sit out of
sight and wait for the monkeys to come. Soon they arrive and
pop their hands through the hole to grab a fistful of nuts.
However, when they try to take their prize catch back to the
safety of the tree, the monkeys cannot get free because the
shape of the hand coming out of the coconut is now bigger
than that which entered. The animals will try all they can to
take out their hands and go free, but they will continue to fail.
It is quite obvious that for the monkeys to go free they must
do one simple thing, that is, to let go, but invariably they will
not because they prefer to hang on to their possessions even if
it means the possibility of losing their freedom!

Likewise, when we refuse to forgive, we then hang on to the

issues, or desires for retribution, which will ultimately destroy our freedom to live a full and wholesome life. This was well-illustrated some years ago when I preached on forgiveness at a celebration service in a Methodist church in Cheshire. At the end of the sermon I invited people to be quiet in the presence of the Lord and allow him an opportunity to make us aware if we held an unforgiving attitude towards anyone or any particular event or issue which had hurt us and which still held us in some way in its grip. When each person had been made aware of anything by God I suggested that they closed their right hand into a fist, as a way of focusing their attention on the fact of what it was they had been holding against anyone down the years or months. Then when they were ready, I encouraged them to raise their right hand into the air and slowly but deliberately open their hand as a way of indicating to God that they were letting go in his name of whatever they had harboured against another. This also reminded them that it was by the grace of God that they could do this meaningfully and with real healing consequences. Where there was any need of confession or repentance they were to do this quietly before God, and should they require further counsel then to follow up their work accordingly.

Afterwards an elderly married couple came forward to talk to me and to share what had happened for them. The husband was clearly upset and began by telling me that he had been uncomfortable during the service because he thought he had been coming to a musical. When he turned to complain to his wife about this, to his surprise he saw that she had her right hand, closed like a fist, up in the air. 'What are you doing that for?' he had asked. 'I'm letting go of you', was the reply! His wife went on to tell him that she had found their thirty years of marriage very hard going because he was full of bitterness and never ceased to criticize everything which she did. Over the years she had nursed deep resentment towards him but that night she had started down the road of forgiveness.

What was so challenging was that the husband said he had held a bitter grievance against his sister who always complained about what he did and the final straw for him had been the way she had criticized his choice of wife. He decided at that moment never to see or speak to his sister again if he could help it, and as far as I know he had kept to his decision. Now the horrible truth had dawned upon him, the very thing which he had held against his sister had become his possession, his very self. That moment of awareness had broken his pride as, at the back of the church, he said sorry to his wife and then very deliberately he too held up his right hand in a fist and asked the Lord to help him let go of his sister. For him that work of letting go took him down the road to a personal commitment to Jesus Christ as his Lord and saviour.

The letting go of forgiveness is dynamic in the sense that it is an activity we are called upon to do, or to take and receive from another. There is nothing passive about experiencing forgiveness, it must be grasped to be given and grasped to be received. It is therefore confessional in nature because to offer it we must be aware of what we have taken as hurt and what we have held against the other which we need to release. For the recipient it is also confessional because it involves repentance which is the action needed to accept the rightness of our need to be forgiven and also the impetus to change and possibly offer some reconciling action to heal the relationship with the one we have offended, as well as with ourselves. A tough work of love indeed; no wonder James Denney describes it as follows:

> There is no forgiveness which is painless, cheap or easy. There is always passion in it on both sides: a passion of penitence on the one side, and the more profound passion of love on the other, bearing the sin of the guilty to him, through reconciliation, to goodness again.[15]

However, we need to sound a cautionary word here about the content and the process of forgiveness. We must not be too hasty to conclude that forgiveness in some mysterious way eradicates our problems or itself brings a change in our behaviour. When we consider words like *kaphar* (to cover) we see that forgiveness does not mean a denial of the past as if it never was. Rather, it means the removal of the effects of the past on the present. It is as if through forgiveness God has removed what has blocked our view of the way into wholeness for us. We are now set upon a road of healing and we must make the most of God's grace to rebuild any ruined place within our lives. John Owen said, in his classic exposition of Psalm 130, that there were three basic results from the personal discovery of forgiveness which would open up the possibility of true spiritual growth. The first was a resolution to abide wholeheartedly in God. He wrote, 'I am resolved to abide in the gospel desire and expectation of it all the days of my life; here my choice is fixed and will not alter.'[16] The second was a resolution to wait on God for peace and consolation, and the third was an ability to receive deliverance out of any future pressures which may occur.

So we can see that forgiveness is never an end in itself, a cul-de-sac of blessing and good will to others. It is rather a doorway of opportunity through which much healing and release is to be found. Also it will make demands of us which will undoubtedly involve us in repentance and personal renewal. We shall be made to feel uncomfortable because we are being called to walk with God at his pace and in the bright light of his grace. It will make us feel vulnerable and scared and we shall have to battle with our sharply felt feelings, our guilt and our memories which will from time to time make us want to run and hide or not to forgive because it feels safer. It was the Reverend J. Spooner of spoonerism fame who, when desiring to describe the pastoral heart of his Lord, said that the Lord is my shoving leopard! The forgiveness of God will feel as though we have got a leopard by the tail and are being pulled out of our comfortable routines to face up to things from which we may have been running all our lives. Yet we shall be more alive than ever before and we will be discovering that only in the action of forgiveness is there the freedom to discover our true potential for being creative and Christ-like.

Before we explore in more depth some of the healing results of this forgiveness we shall spend a little time examining just who it is that has been commissioned and called to be a forgiver and something of the costliness and challenge which result from carrying it through.

Forgiveness for Jesus was not just something to do with being God. It said something profound about being truly human.[17]

2

The Power to Forgive

*One longs to see the church becoming in modest, minor,
broken ways, something of a paradigm, a model . . . of
what grace can bring about, a fellowship of the 'unlike'
able to speak to the world of the possibility of genuine
reconciliation and justice because its members have begun
to realise in their own life together the radical implications
of God's reconciliation.*

Simon Barrington-Ward[1]

Jesus expected his disciples to be forgivers. What is also important is that he did not regard this as an option but a commitment.
This is certainly implied by the commissioning account which
John gives in his Gospel. Jesus appears to his assembled followers in the upper room and he prefaces his introduction to
the ministry of forgiveness with a reminder that they are to be
sent out in the same way in which his heavenly father had sent
him out (John 20:21). Then he 'breathed on them' which can
at least be taken as a reference or pointer towards the moment
when the Holy Spirit would come upon them in power. What
is important, however, is that Jesus couples the giving of the
Spirit with the work of forgiveness. It also tells us that for
forgiveness to be effective and real it has to be the result of
divine grace and not just human inclination. Being born of the
Spirit, and also filled with the Spirit, will inevitably result in
works of forgiveness. As Jim Graham says, 'As children of
God, we are more like our Father when we forgive; and that
as we choose to forgive so God the Holy Spirit comes alongside
us to enable us to make it real.'[2]

There are two cameo moments I would like to examine which confirm how the early Church took its role of forgiver seriously. The first comes from Peter's bold response to persecution from the party of the Saduccees who had had the apostles thrown into jail. He defended their ministry on the grounds that they were simply carrying out as witnesses what they had seen to be the ministry of Jesus. Peter said:

> The God of our fathers raised Jesus from the dead – whom you had killed by hanging him on a tree. God exalted him to his own right hand as Prince and Saviour that he might give repentance and forgiveness of sins to Israel. We are witnesses to these things, and so is the Holy Spirit, whom God gives to those who obey him. (Acts 5:30–2)

Peter is saying amongst other things that forgiveness is at the disposal of Christ but because the Church is witness, or participator in his ministry, then it too is a channel for forgiveness. Of course we must also remind ourselves that the Church had some good models of this stance of intercessory forgiveness in the lives of some of the Old Testament saints. Consider, for example, the way in which Moses stood before God on the mountain and pleaded with God not to destroy the Israelites because of the idolatrous calf they had made (Exodus 32:30–3). In so standing before God, Moses both identified with the sins of his people as well as proclaimed that there was forgiveness with God. Also, there are the great prayers of men like Ezra, Jeremiah and Daniel who, though not involved at all in the sins of the nation, nonetheless prayed, 'O Lord, we have sinned against you.'[3] So we can see that this intermediary ministry of forgiveness is not given from the place of denunciation but from identification.

The second passage to bear in mind is found in Paul's letter to the Colossian church and forms part of the teaching he gives on the dynamics of personal relationships between individuals within the church itself.

> Therefore, as God's chosen people, holy and dearly loved, clothe yourself with compassion, kindness, humility, gentle-

ness and patience. Bear with each other and forgive whatever grievances you may have against one another. Forgive as the Lord forgave you. (Colossians 3:12–13)

Once again, Jesus is the model, this time for the healing of relationships. It is also a reminder to us that our actions have indeed caused a great deal of pain to Jesus, but he chooses not to hold such hurt feelings against us. This was supremely realized in his great words from the cross: 'Father forgive them for they do not know what they are doing' (Luke 23:34). Our forgiveness is gift and undeserved and therefore our offer of it should not be dependent upon the actions, merits or demerits of the one who stands in the need of forgiveness. As we shall see later, to forgive in this way is not easy and is very controversial, but we can only engage in it if we keep going back to that man of Calvary and identifying with his cross and his grace given from it and through it. Some great and famous words on this are those of Emil Brunner who wrote:

In the cross of Christ God says to man, 'That is where you ought to be. Jesus my Son hangs there in your stead. His tragedy is the tragedy of your life. You are the rebel who should be hanged on the gallows. But lo, I suffered instead of you, and because of you, because I love you in spite of what you are. My love is so great that I meet you there, there on the cross. I cannot meet you anywhere else. You must meet me there by identifying yourself with the One on the cross. It is by this identification that I, God, can meet you in Him, saying to you as I say to Him, My beloved Son.'[4]

A brave testimony to this calibre of forgiving is that of the first church martyr, Stephen. He was a gifted communicator and doubtless a powerful witness to the risen Christ; his public witness is rudely interrupted as the crowds drag him out of the city precincts to execute him by stoning. Quite deliberately Stephen imitates the final words of Jesus when he says, 'Lord Jesus, receive my spirit . . . do not hold this sin against them' (Acts 7:59–60). It is quite significant that it is Luke who records the similar dying words of both Jesus and Stephen. He goes on to tell the effects of such an act of forgiveness, for such it was, upon the life of the young zealous Jew called Saul of Tarsus. Jim Graham says that Stephen's courageous act of forgiveness created the space in which God could act in the life of Saul.[5] Whilst this is not directly mentioned, there is the obvious implication that Saul was deeply affected by what he saw. Indeed, it seems more than likely that he was angered and distressed at this offer of forgiveness and set about repressing its conviction in his life by ardently seeking to extinguish the flame of Christianity. Surely this is why, when he heard the voice of Jesus asking him, 'Why do you persecute me?' his immediate response was to acknowledge that he was in the presence of the Lord (Acts 9:4–6).

The commitment to be a forgiver is further enhanced when we look at the prayer which Jesus himself taught those who would follow him. The words are no doubt very familiar to us: 'Forgive us our debts, as we also forgive our debtors' (Matthew 6:12). The word for 'debts' is *opheilemata*; the related verb means 'to be in debt to someone or fail to give a person their due'. This can refer to those many times we fail to appreciate other people's contributions to our lives or fail to acknowledge what we have adopted from their ideas or activities. In other words, we steal their creativity which can form such a barrier between us and even deter the other from growth. Rita Bennett points out that the word for our forgiving is *ophekamen* and is in the past tense.[6] Therefore we are encouraged to receive from God that which we have already completed offering to another. In the Matthean version the prayer is immediately backed up with further teaching on this subject. The disciple is left in no doubt that failure to forgive results in forgiveness being withheld from us by God (Matthew 6:14–15). This is surely what is implied in the passage where we are exhorted that when it comes to our knowledge that another Christian has a grievance against us because of something we may have done, we are to stop what we are doing and make it our top priority to be reconciled and restored to that other member of the Christian Church (Matthew 5:23–4). Matthew writes of leaving our gift at the altar and then going to heal whatever hurts the other has. I often think this means that we may well be called by God to put aside our charismatic gift or ministry, or to lay down our role in the church, as the first step to healing and restoration. If we persist in ignoring the breach in our relationship then it is only a matter of time before God removes his anointing and blessing from our ministry.

Some years ago when I was an incumbent of a church in the Midlands I witnessed a tremendous healing between two brothers. One of the two men, whom I shall call Peter, was an officer in my church and was really keen to get involved in the healing ministry. He encouraged me in my work and was present at the healing services where he eagerly prayed for others to be healed. However, he grew despondent because not only did he not see the healings he hoped for but he grew increasingly restless in his heart. One day I was conducting an ecumenical healing service and Peter was duly sitting up at the front of the church. Without warning, he interrupted my little sermon by sharing his story. He said that he had been realizing more and more over the years just how much he had been angry with God about the lack of encouragement in his life. However, he had begun to realize also that deep in his heart there was a root of bitterness. He told us all as we sat there in the building, gripped by his honesty, how he hated his younger brother. His mother had died when he was nine years old and later on his father had remarried. He felt that his father had stopped loving him and that all the love now went to the new child born, his younger brother Sammy. During his talk, at some point the church door opened and a stranger came in and quietly sat down at the back. Yet when Peter continued his story this man became more and more agitated until he got to his feet and shouted out, 'Peter! It's me!' Peter stopped dead in his tracks; his younger brother had come home on a visit and had been listening to his confession. 'O no!' said Peter, 'I've been telling everybody how much I've hated you.' His brother said he knew all the time. Then they got out of their pews and came and embraced each other in the aisle of the church. For the first time in their lives they were forgiving and healing one another.

The story did not end there. At six o'clock the next morning, which was Easter Day, I had a telephone call from Peter. He said that he and his wife had been kept awake all night as they had been filled with the Holy Spirit and literally had sat up in bed praising God as waves of love seemed to wash over them. He very much wanted to share his testimony with the church at the main Easter Communion service. This was usually an all-too-solemn affair and I was by no means too comfortable with the idea. However, I agreed, and Peter duly came to the front of the church and summarized his story of the night before. He told the packed church that he had learned to forgive and love again, and that this was a good day for us to do the same. He told everyone how much he loved them and said sorry for being difficult at times. On the way back to his seat someone began to clap and most of the congregation joined in. We were being healed through an act of forgiveness. Thanks be to God. God keeps his word and we may need to realize that the reason we do not see growth in our lives and ministry could be because our lives are full with an unforgiving heart.

So we can see that forgiveness is a ministry and a discipline that has been uniquely given to the Church and that it took its role of witness very seriously. Interestingly enough the role of Church as mediator was strongly advocated by the Reformers, and for Calvin, at least, this also included the ministry of confession.

> To impart to us this benefit (forgiveness experienced daily), the keys of the church have been given. When Christ gave the command to the apostles and conferred upon them the power to forgive sins . . . he did not so much desire that the apostles absolve from sins those who might be converted from ungodliness to the faith of Christ, as that they should perpetually discharge this office among believers . . . In the communion of saints, our sins are continually forgiven us by the ministry of the church itself when the presbyters or bishops to whom this office has been committed strengthen consciences by the gospel promises in the hope of pardon and forgiveness. This they do publicly and privately as need

requires . . . And Paul mentions that not only in public preaching but from house to house as well, he has attested his faith in Christ, and has individually admonished each man concerning the doctrine of salvation.[7]

There are two questions which we now need to ask. The first is, who is it in the Church who actually offers this forgiveness to another? Calvin implies that it is the minister who represents the Church in the act of forgiving. This must at least be true, but does this mean that the rest of the Church has no participation in this ministry? Clearly the scriptures teach that we are all involved in this work. This is brought out quite clearly in the Epistle of James which mentions an occasion when the church elders are to be sent for in some circumstances to pray over the sick man (James 5:14). Yet the passage suddenly switches its pace and talks about the need to confess our sins to one another and to pray for one another for healing (5:16). Immediately we have been taken from the presbyterial leadership to the involvement of the whole church. This is surely the emerging conviction as we read through the Gospels and see how Jesus began with twelve and then shared the same commission with the seventy, and finally inaugurated the great commission which essentially was to train the whole Church to engage in everything which the original twelve had been taught.[8] Therefore we need to note that those who represent us within the Church are not there to replace us but to resource us to do our part as and when required.

In order for us to have confidence in our calling to share the great offer of forgiveness we need to remind ourselves that we have been given two great gifts to motivate us. When Jesus sent out the first twelve to preach the gospel of the kingdom, to heal and to deliver from demonic entanglement, he gave them power and authority to do so. This is of course another reminder that the ability to forgive is not ours, it is God's alone, but that we have been called to be channels for such healing. The word for power is *dunamis*, and reflects the sheer energy and power of God to achieve his goals. It is this power which we have been promised when we receive the gift of the

Holy Spirit in our lives (Acts 1:8). With relevance to the issue of forgiveness, therefore, *dunamis* speaks of God's power to set free and heal, and confirms our place as believers to be a channel and a recipient of such power. The word for authority is *exousia*, and speaks more of our right to be standing in this place of ministry. I remember many years ago when I was caught speeding in a little Fiat 500. Seemingly from nowhere I was suddenly confronted by a diminutive-sized policewoman who stood in the middle of the road and held up her hand to signal me to stop. I slammed on my brakes immediately! Yet it must be said that I didn't stop the car because she was bigger than me or looked like giving me some physical pain. I am in fact well over six feet in height and to some degree hovered above her when I got out of the car. The reason I stopped so obediently was because she represented the law of the land and had the authority to prosecute me to the full extent of that law should she have thought it necessary. Such authority was to be respected and it had absolutely nothing to do with her size, looks or ability. So it is for the Christian in caring. We are not engaged in this ministry because we are strong enough or big enough, but because we have the Lord's authority and he will support us to the full extent of his power and presence. However, it is so important that we use both gifts and not just one. So often we will be tempted to feel that because we have so many problems of our own we are not worthy or able to be engaged in such ministry. It is the gift of authority which will say to us it is true that we have problems of our own but by God's grace we have been made a member of his family and have therefore a perfect right to be involved in the work of our elder brother Jesus. It is the gift of power which reminds us that we so much need to rely on the Holy Spirit to work through our weaknesses and to translate our actions into his signs and wonders.

The second question we need to ask is, what is the difference between public and private forgiveness? Here we are perhaps differentiating between proclaiming the forgiveness of sins within an evangelistic setting and enabling an individual, whether a believer or not, to find forgiveness within a confessional or counselling context. This latter circumstance has become much more prominent within the evangelical and charismatic ministries of the Church. There has been an explosion of healing and counselling ministries, much of which refers to inner healing or healing of the memories. Prominent among the routes to wholeness is the need to be set free from the old, crippling agenda of the past, and the prime resource for this is to forgive and be forgiven. In the opinion of Paul Halmos, in his book *The Faith of the Counsellors*, counselling has in fact usurped the place of the confessional and the traditional form of pastoral care from the minister. It has caused, to some degree, a suspicion between pastors and counsellors especially when the former may not have received any formal training in counselling skills. Yet it must also be said that the word 'counsellor' is rather a cheap commodity at present because it is a term used by almost anybody to describe the work of helping another. Unfortunately there are many Christians who use the term and who have had no training at all; their reply is that they much prefer to rely on the initiatives of the Holy Spirit. Whilst I do not want to undermine the absolute necessity for doing this, I sometimes feel this has become a stock phrase for doing what I feel is right. Sadly the casualties from an undisciplined and untrained venture in counselling are all too obvious and, for many, Christian care has therefore obtained a murky reputation. However, there are growing signs that the Church is beginning to take the role of counselling seriously and now many more theological colleges include some form of training in skills on their curriculum. Added to this is the growing desire amongst Christians to make sure that Christian counselling is properly assessed and accredited.[9]

I think it is important that we underline and be confident in our calling as the Church of Jesus Christ to make people aware of the possibility of forgiveness, both for those who as yet stand outside a committed faith and for those who need personal counsel and direction. And of course it is not only a ministry to offer for the benefit of others, it is to be our daily practice for our journey through life also. I well remember the elder of a house church in Manchester many years ago telling me of how God had suddenly challenged him on his lack of real forgiveness. I had been preaching on the subject of father and sons and during the course of my sermon his mind had drifted back to an occasion when he was about nine years old (he was now in his fifties) when his father had slapped him for something he had done wrong. He even remembered how painful it had felt, but he was more pained by a second memory which now lined up alongside the first. He remembered when he had been converted some twenty years later and shortly afterwards was vigorously witnessing to his father about his need to be saved. He thought about how his father felt very uncomfortable to be challenged in this way, and John had rather enjoyed the feeling it gave him to see this. He said, 'It felt like getting my own back for that time when he punished me.' However, sitting through my sermon God began to show him that because of his revengeful attitude, his father had not really heard the Good News but had just felt harassed. John's father had still not become a Christian despite nearly thirty years of witnessing to him. He felt quite convicted by this revelation and later went home and apologized to his Dad for the way he had made him feel all those years ago and asked his Dad to forgive him. I am happy to report that this was a turning-point and that John's father, who remembered his son's witness and attitude quite clearly, was deeply moved and later gave his life to the Lord Jesus.

FORGIVENESS IS COSTLY

Many of us will remember the incredible witness of Gordon Wilson concerning his forgiveness towards members of the IRA who were responsible for bombing his teenage daughter Marie to death. Gordon, a layman in the Methodist Church, was attending the Remembrance Day parade in Enniskillen in November 1987 when, without warning, a bomb went off amongst those attending the parade, killing eleven people. Gordon himself was injured and lay under a pile of rubble holding his daughter's hand until she said that she was hurting quite badly, that she loved her daddy, and then let go of his hand and died. His calm and dignified witness to his love for his daughter and his God impressed millions of people who watched his interview on prime-time television. He honestly said that he did not understand why it had happened but he believed that it was part of God's bigger plan. He and his wife Joan missed their daughter terribly but he said that he would pray every day for those who had killed her because he had been taught as a Christian that he was to forgive others as he would have them forgive him.

This one act of forgiveness caught the public imagination and Gordon was both hailed as a remarkable man and attacked for being too lenient. Apparently he received three hundred thousand letters of sympathy, and that Christmas the Queen made his act of forgiveness the basis of her message. However, Janet Street-Porter, in her newspaper column, warned her readers about the dangers of an all-too-easy and speady forgiveness as it bottled up resentments with disastrous psychological results. She insisted that Gordon Wilson's forgiveness had brought about a nervous breakdown.[10] Yet it seems much more likely that the horrific murder of his daughter was more stressful than his life-long practice of forgiveness. In a magazine programme called *Friday Night Live* on Central Television in 1991, Gordon Wilson was again in front of the cameras. Alongside him was the mother of Leslie Ann Downey, a young girl murdered by Myra Hindley and Ian Brady in what has become known as the infamous Moors murders. Once again Gordon Wilson expressed his forgiveness towards the members of the IRA, but he was followed by Leslie's mother who, still full of grief at the death and disappearance of her daughter, said that it was her hatred which had kept her alive and that she thought it was unchristian and wrong to forgive people like Brady and Hindley, as well as the terrorists. Neither was she pacified when told that Myra Hindley in particular had shown real repentance and remorse at what she had done and was now fully co-operating with the authorities to recover the bodies of the children who had been buried somewhere on Saddleworth Moor near Oldham. Hindley had also embraced the Catholic faith and was genuinely seeking forgiveness and restoration. However, for this distraught mother it seemed that Christian forgiveness was tantamount to allowing the criminals to escape and her be stuck with the pain of a murdered daughter.

In one sense this form of controversy is not too difficult to understand or respond to as a Christian. For some there is real concern that the offer of forgiveness may sweep issues like justice and punishment under the carpet. These are discussed very well in Richard Rice-Oxley's Grove Book called *Forgiveness – The Way of Peace*. He quotes the quotable C. S. Lewis who points out the difference between forgiveness and excusing:

> There is all the difference in the world between forgiving and excusing. Forgiveness says, 'Yes, you have done this thing, but I accept your apology, I will never hold it against you and everything between us two will be exactly as it was before.' But excusing says, 'I see that you couldn't help it, or didn't mean it, you weren't really to blame.' If one was not really to blame then there is nothing to forgive. In that sense forgiveness and excusing are almost opposite.[11]

So forgiveness is not an either-or situation. We can truly forgive but not necessarily be committed to suspending the law of crime and punishment. What is more difficult to handle is the animosity towards the offer of forgiveness. Jesus was crucified on the cross partly because he was a forgiver of other peoples' sins. The scribes and the Pharisees both questioned Jesus' authority to forgive, but more importantly they disagreed with his attitude towards forgiveness. Jesus forgave too extravagantly for their liking and seemed not to be too concerned about laying down rules of penitence. This was not because he was not concerned with holiness of life and restitution, but was more a demonstration of his belief that to receive forgiveness is in itself an indication of a desire to change and that forgiveness gives the space and opportunity to change. There was an intolerance in them about the route that led to repentance and Jesus was breaking their rules. It was rather like a power game where Jesus' forgiveness freed the person not only from their sinful life but also from the domination of the Pharisees.

Similarly, we will encounter hostility and spiritual warfare when we proclaim forgiveness to those bound in unforgiveness. The powers of darkness cannot remain where forgiveness and redemption have been applied. It should be no surprise that immediately following the command to forgive others in the Lord's Prayer is the injunction to be freed from temptation and delivered from evil. Forgiveness challenges and explodes the domination of the powers of darkness in our lives, be those spiritual or temporal. We become free to change and choose a new future. This is why David Runcorn is right when he says that to be forgiven is to have your life shaken up. And this is just as true for nations as for individuals. Just as something must die for forgiveness to be offered, supremely the sacrifice of Jesus upon the cross, so also something must die for forgiveness to be received.[12] What needs to die in us is perhaps the power of the old order of living in exchange for the new order of release and hope in Jesus.

Another reason for hostility towards this ministry is because of what forgiveness points towards, and that is both an awareness of the problem and the need to change. Therefore to realize the need to be forgiven is a form of conviction and exposure of our sinful actions and our total inability to do anything to earn or gain it. This can be decidedly uncomfortable! The temptation is all too real to rebel or go to into denial of need. John White gives a good example of this form of denial and animosity in a story he tells from the days when he was working in a hospital as a psychiatrist. He was working with a forty-year-old male patient who had already spent several weeks on the psychiatric ward of a general hospital. He believed that he had cancer and that the authorities were lying to him when they told him that he showed no evidence of it. He had no energy, no appetite and he couldn't sleep. He was given antipsychotic pills and antidepressants, all of which left him unchanged. He also had ten electro-convulsive treatments. Still no change.

Later he began to talk about his life and he referred to two 'sins', the first was drinking a bottle of beer in defiance of his doctor's orders; secondly, and more significantly, he had avoided enlistment in World War II and felt guilty because some of his friends had died in Europe. Somewhere during the conversation John White raised the issue of forgiveness. He wanted it so badly but felt totally unworthy or unable to accept it, this despite knowing at one level that Christ had died for his sins and shed his blood so that he could be forgiven.

'I'm too bad for that', he said. Unaccountably I grew angry (writes John). No logical reason. It just happened. 'What do you mean you're too bad?' His voice was rising like my own, 'I don't deserve to be forgiven.' 'You're darn right you don't!' He looked at me surprised. 'I can't be a hypocrite. I gotta make amends.' It may be hard to believe, but I found my anger increasing. 'And who do you think you are to say that Christ's death was not good enough for you? Who are you to feel you must add your miserable pittance to the great gift God offers you? Is his sacrifice not good enough for the likes of you?'

This man was stunned, and then he began to cry and pray as the impact of what he had heard spoke to the blockage within his heart. It was a cathartic moment; though initially he had resented it, he now suddenly saw the power of it and it saved him. John White goes on to report that all medication was eventually cut out, his paranoia vanished and he recovered from the depths of his depression. In later dialogue he said that the turning-point was when he realized that although he saw his need of forgiveness he had nonetheless despised the offer of God's mercy through Christ.[13]

Ever since the day of Pentecost, therefore, the Church has received this divine mandate to proclaim the forgiveness of sins through Jesus Christ and to practise its own preaching both within its ranks and to the world around it. This is the Calvary stance of the Church, which is to its dear cost, and yet also a powerful resource for the healing of persons and nations, as we shall see. As James Emerson wrote, when he was commenting on Bonhoeffer's concept of costly grace:

Pastor Bonhoeffer wrote that the cost of discipleship is obedience. It is not. The real cost of discipleship is to accept forgiveness – and that is a genuine sacrifice.[14]

3

Forgiveness and Salvation

*To speak the word of pardon, to blot out the past and open
up the future, to give peace of conscience, to impart hope
to the broken and launch them in the career of loving their
neighbour as themselves – nothing else could be so great.*

H. R. Mackintosh[1]

Perhaps the most significant form of healing which forgiveness
brings is that of salvation. A graphic and powerful illustration
of this connection between forgiveness and salvation can be
found in the film *The Mission*, directed by Roland Joffe. The
story focuses on the lives of a slave-trader called Rodrigo Mendoza and Father Gabriel who witnesses amongst natives and
colonizers alike. Mendoza kills his younger brother in an angry
duel because his brother wins the love of his own mistress. Yet
afterwards he is full of remorse and pain but is totally unable
to find relief or peace of mind. Consequently his unforgiving
state drags him down into drunkenness and despair. It is Father
Gabriel who tells him of the forgiveness and salvation that
await him if he turns towards God. However, for Mendoza, it
all seems too easy and consequently too far from his grasp.
Then comes a moment of insight by which he sees how he may
receive the free gift of forgiveness. Father Gabriel is about to
return to work amongst the natives in the mountains and Mendoza insists on joining them.

There follows the remarkable scene of Mendoza scaling the
cliffs, but behind him he drags a huge baggage consisting of all
the weapons of his former occupation of slave-trader. He is
doing penance in a highly symbolic fashion and, like Christian

in Bunyan's *Pilgrim's Progress*, he carries his burden until the moment of release. Perhaps this helps us to see that forgiveness is both an event and a process. Mendoza carries his burden because he knows that he can be forgiven and has been offered forgiveness by the act of God's free grace. Yet the full impact or ability to receive it is still to come. His penance reveals how much he desires it and how much he is unworthy and unable to achieve it.

Eventually, Mendoza reaches the top of the mountains and lies dirty and exhausted on the ground; but still he has no relief for his guilt. The Indians instantly recognize the man whom they hate and fear. One of them rushes over to the prostrate figure and takes out his knife and lifts up Mendoza's head; Mendoza simply accepts the situation and awaits death. It is a tremendous moment of tension. Suddenly the knife comes down and the huge baggage is released and falls off the cliff top. Immediately the slave-trader is no longer the slave; he realizes that the Indians have forgiven him his many murders, and so he breaks down with relief into tears and laughter. It is at this point that, according to David Runcorn, Mendoza enters the fellowship of the forgiven.[2] It is acceptance by the Amazonian Indians which conveys to Mendoza that he has also been forgiven by God; this he can receive.

This story well illustrates for us the scriptural picture that salvation is a healing encounter with God because it opens the door to creative change and growth. There are in fact six dimensions or relationships to these healing changes:

1   My relationship with God.
2   My relationship with myself.
3   My relationship with others.
4   My relationship with the past.
5   My relationship with the present.
6   My relationship with the future.

Before exploring these relationships we shall first examine how salvation is revealed in the New Testament as a healing experience.

In Luke's Gospel there is the account of the ten lepers who

cried out for Jesus to heal them. He instructs them to go to the priests for inspection, but on the way to the temple they are suddenly healed (Luke 17:15–19). However, only one actually returns to thank Jesus, and in doing so he falls at his feet to acknowledge that Jesus is Lord. Incidentally, we are told that the man who came back praising was a Samaritan who, according to popular Jewish conviction, would have been unlikely to receive the blessings of God. God's ways still have not changed, thankfully. Luke's account draws together two interesting words both of which describe what has happened to the leper. First he realizes that he has been healed (17:15). The word here is *iaomai* which usually means 'be healed' or 'restored to health'. It is a word which comes from a medical background. It occurs twenty times in the Gospels and the majority are to be found in the Gospel of Luke. This should not surprise us as Luke is known as an *iatros*, or physician (Colossians 4:14). Jesus' final words are 'Rise and go; your faith has saved you' (Luke 17:19, Jerusalem Bible). The second word is *sodzo*, and it comes from a word which means 'to be safe'. It basically became identified with God's acts of deliverance for his people from danger, disease and death, both physical and spiritual. Consequently, it is understood as the word for salvation in the New Testament. Foerster, in speaking of God's salvation, concludes from the use of this word that salvation is an act of healing the whole person.[3] For the leper, the first encounter with Jesus brought him physical healing, he was cleansed of his leprosy; the second encounter brought him salvation, he was made whole.

There are other examples in the Gospels of how this word is used to illustrate this linking of salvation with healing. William Tyndale, in translating the words of Jesus to Zacchaeus says, 'Today health has come to your home' (Luke 19:9). This emphasizes the fact that this man who was looking for Jesus received healing not only in his spiritual life but in his emotions and his relationships. Consider, for example, the immediate response he makes when Jesus enters his home with the gift of salvation: he gives half his possessions to the poor and pays back those he had defrauded by four times the amount concerned (Luke 19:8).

Another good example is the story of the woman who had spent all her money in trying to be healed from some form of internal haemorrhaging. She nervously threaded her way through the crowds which thronged around Jesus and, lowering herself down, barely met him as she touched the hem of his garment (Luke 8:42–8). But, as we know, Jesus, through his incredible awareness, felt her contact and the need and purpose behind it. As soon as she touched Jesus, we are told that the condition from which she was suffering ceased; she was healed of her complaint. However, when Jesus eventually spoke to her he told her that her faith had saved her or made her whole. At first she had a healing, but now she is whole because she confessed her need of Christ and in that was the faith which made her whole. So we can conclude from these examples that salvation is also healing because it demonstrates God's commitment to make us whole and to restore our relationship with him through Jesus Christ our Lord.

1 FORGIVENESS AND RESTORING MY RELATIONSHIP WITH GOD

Dietrich Bonhoeffer wrote:

> Cheap grace is the preaching of forgiveness without requiring repentance, baptism without church discipline, communion without confession, absolution without personal confession. Cheap grace is grace without discipleship, grace without the cross, grace without Jesus Christ, living and incarnate.[4]

Forgiveness is healing because it enables the healing of my relationship with God and this is to be truly saved.

> Our sin is that we fail to acknowledge our need and dependence upon God, our need to be in a state of reconciliation with our Creator and all that is good in his creation. It is setting up ourselves on our own, claiming to be the masters of our own destiny (pride) and to be our own gods (idolatry).[5]

We are in a state of alienation and the principal route of return for us is to come to the place where we want and do receive the forgiveness of a loving God and father. It is this determination and desire for forgiveness which is often the hallmark of God's work to bring us into the joy of his salvation. John Owen, the Puritan preacher who was chaplain to Oliver Cromwell, pointed out the difference between awareness of sin and acknowledgement of sin: 'Men may have a sense of sin, and yet suffer it to lie burning as a fire shut up in their bones, to their continual disquietude, without coming to a free, soul-opening acknowledgement.'[6] He goes on to contrast the different results of awareness and acknowledgement of sin. There is a telling illustration of this between verses 3 and 5 of Psalm 32. Verse 3 recounts how David felt about his sins: 'When I kept silent, my bones wasted away through my groaning all day long.' Yet notice the change of mood when he confesses his sins: 'Then I acknowledged my sin to you and did not cover up my iniquity. I said, "I will confess my transgressions to the Lord" – and you forgave the guilt of my sin' (verse 5). The acknowledgement of sin is perhaps the first step we take on the road to forgiveness, and reflects that the Holy Spirit is at work in us to convict us of our sins and lead us into righteousness.

So we can see that the obtaining of forgiveness is no casual pursuit. Real salvation is signalled by a deep determination to find forgiveness for our sins and to be found in a right relationship with God. As Emil Brunner says:

> The perfect revelation of forgiveness can only be such as brings out with intense emphasis that it cannot and must not be taken for granted. This means it must be of such a kind that it will express the reality of guilt, the reality of the divine wrath, and yet, at the same time the overwhelming reality of forgiving love.[7]

In other words, we simply cannot take the forgiveness of God for granted in a cheap and assuming way. Our desire for it and its power within us are directly proportional to our awareness of the gulf by which our sins separate us from God.

We have already referred to the story of the woman who came into Simon the Pharisee's house, seeking out Jesus. The Good News version of the Bible describes her as 'a well-known woman from the district' (Luke 7:37). Think of her ordeal and determination as she had to battle her way through the condemnation and disdain of a men-only group! Yet Jesus, in referring to her frosty reception, makes up a story about someone who will love much because they have been forgiven much. In other words, this woman was so stirred up about the need of forgiveness that she was determined not to let anything stop her finding it. For Jesus, there was a release of love within her because she knew that her sins, which were many, had been forgiven.

There is no inconsistency in the heart of God when he reveals the depth of our sins and at the same time shows us the gift of forgiveness.

> Love, that is worthy to be called love, confronts the evil thing with an inevitable purity. If God did not chastise sin in the very act of forgiveness, and in the persons of the forgiven as a sequel to forgiving them, He would be no more loving than He is; He would cease to be God.[8]

Therefore our need to press after forgiveness is a good indication that God is challenging us to come to know him as Father and Lord. For John Owen, it is the focusing on forgiveness rather than on the sins committed which is the real signal that a work of salvation has begun in the human heart:

> Pressing after forgiveness is the very life and power of evangelical humiliation. How shall a man know that his humiliation is evangelical, that his sorrow is according to God? He does not do as Cain did, who cried his sins were greater than he could bear, and so departed from the presence of God; nor as Judas did, who repented, and hanged himself; nor as Felix did, tremble for a while, and then return to his lusts; but in the midst of it all he applies himself to God in Christ for pardon and mercy. *It is the soul's application unto God*

for forgiveness, and not its sense of sin, that gives to God the glory of his grace.[9]

This journey into receiving forgiveness has four basic steps or stopping places; they are repentance, confession, reconciliation and restoration. In reality of course we cannot so rigidly separate these experiences as they can be so easily telescoped into one moment when the grace of God invades our lives with a life-changing encounter. This is I suppose the way I came to salvation. When I was just twenty, like many of my peers, my life more or less consisted of social drinking and not much else. As far as I am aware there was no real interest or belief in the Christian gospel, nor our saviour Jesus Christ. However, there came an evening when I was wandering rather aimlessly around the streets of Birkenhead when I chanced to go into what was called a coffee bar. I think I must have heard the rock and roll music (with suitable Christian lyrics of course) that was being played and curiosity took me inside. I was aware that I began to feel uncomfortable, but for some reason chose to stay for a while. Eventually I sat down next to a man who didn't look at all like my apochryphal picture of a Christian – suits, short hair and ties! He was rather large and extremely unkempt and smoked rather heavily, as I recall.

Shortly afterwards, and after we had engaged in small talk, I announced that I was leaving but that I knew a pub that was open after hours and I invited him to come with me. He agreed and so we left. We walked down a street and then we stepped over a low wall surrounding a church and began to walk round the church. As the pub was just around the corner of the street I concluded that we were taking a short cut and so didn't give the matter a second thought. However, alarm bells began to go off inside me when it slowly dawned on me that our route was actually taking us to a dead end; this was no short cut. In front of us was a very high wall with broken glass cemented into its ridge. My companion, who was called Fred, said nothing but I suddenly feared that he had brought me here to mug me or something worse. And so I steeled myself for flight. Yet I was not prepared for what came next.

Fred turned to me, and I inwardly stiffened for escape, and then he said, 'I've brought you here to pray with you. You don't mind do you?' 'No', I lied. He then proceeded to kneel down and leaned on a dustbin and prayed for my salvation. The only words I can now remember of that prayer were that he prayed for the blindfold to be removed from around my eyes. That caught my attention and I asked him what he meant. Briefly he told the old, old story that Jesus had died for my sins and that I needed to receive his love and salvation. I wanted to protest my unbelief but it all suddenly melted away in my throat as I powerfully realized that everything he had told me was absolutely true. I have no way of accounting for this or explaining my sudden embrace of the gospel, but it flooded over me and I felt unclean and in need of being made clean. I so much wanted Jesus to be my Lord and Saviour that I had no rest that night until I had committed my life to God.

That happened in 1967 and ever since it has been my privilege and joy to be a disciple of Jesus Christ. However, we cannot make our testimony the norm for others and we need to realize that for others the journey to salvation is often slower and the steps are put together rather differently. I often think of my good friend Hugh who was a librarian in Liverpool and for whom I once worked. He is a kindly and compassionate man whom I am pleased to call my friend, and his fatherly counsel has always been welcome. There came the day when I was finishing working with him in order to go into Bible College to train for the ministry. Hugh called me into his office on that final day and began to tell me how much he had enjoyed working with me. Then he both surprised and delighted me when he said that he wanted to be my friend and especially so because I had helped him to come to know Jesus more personally and that he had been restored in his relationship with God. Now, Hugh had a faith and was familiar with his need for repentance and confession and had practised such for some time. Yet he had not come to that stage in the journey where he knew restoration in his heart with God the Father. This he said had now become real for him, and from then onwards we have enjoyed sharing our love for the Lord as two good friends and brothers in Jesus, despite the fact that he is thirty years older than I am.

So let us look a bit more closely at these steps which bring us into the joy of our salvation.

(a) Repentance

Repentances could be called little resurrections.[10]

The Gospel of Mark begins very starkly and very powerfully with John the Baptist preaching a baptism of repentance for the forgiveness of sins (Mark 1:4). Jesus took up this theme in his public ministry when John had been imprisoned: 'Repent and believe the good news', he proclaimed (Mark 1:15). And it is this same combination of repentance and forgiveness which Jesus hands on to his disciples just prior to his ascension (Luke 24:47). So we can see that repentance and forgiveness stand at the very heart of the kingdom message.[11] Arthur Karney, using the parable of the prodigal son as his analogy, describes repentance as the moment when we decide to return home, and forgiveness as the welcome home by the Father who comes to meet us on our way back.[12]

The New Testament word for repentance is *metanoia* and refers to a change of mind or a complete turning around. Morris Maddocks describes it as a reorientation of the personality.[13] It is both a signal and evidence that the Holy Spirit is at work to open up our lives to the presence of God for us, and hopefully within us. In fact, it is a revolution in awareness. Jesus described it as an experience of conviction which addresses not only our sinful deeds but also our need for righteousness and the judgement to befall us should we fall short of such godly requirements. He said, 'When he comes [that is, the Counsellor, the Spirit], he will convict the world of guilt in regard to sin and righteousness and judgement; in regard to sin, because men do not believe in me; in regard to righteousness, because I am going to the Father . . . and in regard to judgement, because the prince of this world now stands condemned' (John 16:8–11).

John White picks up this theme of repentance as an inner

revolution and describes it as another way of seeing reality. He refers to it as a 'paradigm shift' in which people see themselves in a different light and begin facing truths about themselves which earlier they had denied.[14] Because of the life-changing results of repentance we can conclude that this is no mere moment of emotional turbulence or nostalgia and longing for a better way; it is a fundamental challenge to the way we understand our own personal reality, and affects both thought, feeling and will. If you read the accounts of the revivals under the ministries of both Wesleys and Whitefield in the eighteenth century, you will observe not only deep emotion evidenced by tears but radical change in behaviour long after the emotional fervour has subsided. In other words there is a permanence about the effects of repentance which cannot be said to be sustained by the heights or depths of emotion. There has been a revolution in thinking, willing and living also.

Stanley Banks, who was the Principal of Emmanuel Bible College where I trained for the ministry in the late 1960s, used to say that repentance was like being arrested by God so that we could know both the charges and the offer of acquittal at the same time. Repentance implies a recognition of our guilt and need for forgiveness, and there is no going back to God without it. C. S. Lewis defined repentance as 'simply a description of what going back to him is like. If you ask God to take you back without it, you are really asking him to let you go back without going back. It cannot happen.'[15]

Finally, repentance is never really a private affair. This is perhaps because sin is never really a private affair either. As a counsellor I have listened to those who have been wounded by the lives of those they have lived with. Consider the wife of a man with an alcoholic problem; whilst the husband struggles with his inner issues and the way his drinking masks such things, she has to battle with dwindling resources to keep the family together whilst all the time trying to keep in check her own outraged feelings. For such a man to change radically he has to convince his partner that this is reality and not the temporary regrets of the remorseful and sobering man. He may be faced with cynicism or unbelief and this can be very hard to sum-mount at first. Therefore repentance will inevitably involve the risk of being vulnerable to others, especially those we have wronged. This is surely what the Apostle Paul faced following his conversion. Agreed, there was the generous yet risky response of Ananias who was a bit scared to go and meet the former persecutor of the faithful (Acts 9:13–14); yet there were also those who were not too convinced about Paul's conversion and were all too suspicious for a while (Acts 9:21, 26). It may well be, of course, that we actually need the help of those we have harmed to enable us to regain a new way of living. Where would Paul have been without Ananias and Barnabas? So repentance is also a call for the harmed or offended to forgive and to share in our walk in newness of life. God is the supreme example of this. He freely forgives our sins and restores us in our walk with him and comes alongside us by the Holy Spirit, to help secure a new future of hope for us. This is why Basilea Schlink called repentance the joy-filled life, because it signalled the return to kingdom living.[16] It is the stepping-stone into the Easter life which takes us back both to the cross and to the upper room of the outpoured Spirit.

> At root, repentance is about where we discover the clues to what being human is really about. It says that failure can be redeemed, broken relationships can be healed, a sense of despair can become a cry of hope, that isolation can be transformed into relationship, that dread can be changed into hope.[17]

(b) Confession

If we confess our sins, he is just and may be trusted to forgive our sins and cleanse us from every kind of wrongdoing.

1 John 1:9 (Revised English Bible)

Some years ago now I was a member of renewal prayer group which met in St Joseph's Convent in Upton in the Wirral. It was led by a small group which included Ray Nean, one of the lay leaders, and Sisters Emmanuel and Breda; their love for the Lord Jesus was one of the great encouragers of my growth in God in those days. There was one occasion when we were busily praising God by singing a particular chorus when we were suddenly interrupted by 'Marion' crying out, 'God can't love me!' Initially we continued to sing, thinking that this was only an interruption and would not be repeated. We were wrong. Marion proceeded to cry out all the louder that God could not love her because she did not deserve anything for what she had done. I can remember very clearly how Sister Emmanuel shouted out to the rest of us, 'Shut up, for God's sake! Can't you see that she is trying to confess something?'

During the silence that followed, Marion poured out her story. She said that she was glad the day her mother died because she, being the youngest in the family, had been pressurized by her mother to look after her when she was ill and needed company now that her husband had died. This had dragged on, as she put it, until she was thirty-nine years old. After her mother's death she had married the first man she could get and they had had two sons. However, as each son had reached their eighteenth birthday they had left home. After the last son had left, her husband had abruptly informed her that he too was leaving because she had made his life a hell; she had been far too possessive and domineering. And so she was left alone, stuck with her bitter feelings and regrets. Apparently during the worship she had begun to realize how she had projected her insecurities onto resenting her mother and dominating her family. She felt a sudden need and urge to say so aloud because she wanted to get it out into the open and to be heard. This was her confession.

I am happy to report that due to some sensitive listening to her story by Sister Emmanuel, Marion was able to get out what had been locked up within, and so come to some space where she could receive God's love and salvation for herself. We can see therefore that confession is principally a vocal step of disclosure. Paul wrote in his Epistle to the Romans, 'For it is with the heart that you believe and are justified, and it is with your mouth that you confess and are saved' (Romans 10:10).

This is true not only for that initial experience of salvation but also for all future moments of healing. The act of confession makes clear our need for help and the area of our trespass. It is a time of vulnerability alongside another as we let them hear our story and hope that they, be it God or anyone else we have injured, take our concern to heart with openness, care and forgiveness. In being heard and received we are healed, we begin our journey on the road to wholeness. 'The person expressing penitence hands over the feelings of alienation, despair, impotent rage, powerlessness and apathy, with the clear expectation that they will be set in a radically different context.'[18] Hence the prodigal son not only reminds himself of his sins whilst at his lowest moment amongst the pig-pens, he also confesses the same in the presence of his father. Confession is not confession if it is not heard.

Confession is also a challenge to the Church both to listen to the needs of the community as well as declaring its own need of forgiveness and healing. I think that it is here that the Evangelical can learn something valuable from the Catholic. By this I mean the therapy of the confessional. It was Dame Cicely Saunders, founder of the hospice movement, who said that in a climate of listening people will say more. The confessional is an invitation to the penitent to say more. I remember as an incumbent asking why a certain person was no longer attending the church services. No one really knew and they all made different suggestions. When I eventually went to visit her and asked her myself she said that she had been trying for months to tell me how difficult life had become with her husband but I had always seemed to be too busy to give her the time and the space. So eventually she had given up hope and drifted away. Needless to say, I felt very bad and was convicted of not giving her confessional space to share.

The confessional is not so much an interrogation of our life-styles or an itemizing of our sins, but an opportunity to give space to another so that they can own and disclose those things which stand in the way of obtaining release and forgiveness through Jesus Christ. However, we do need to underline that the confessional is not the same as counselling. Quite often counselling is a discipline by which an individual clarifies how they feel about themselves, whereas to confess is to find the directive route for finding forgiveness with God or another. Inevitably this means coming to the foot of the cross and recognizing that in order to be truly forgiven God has made atonement for the wrongs I have done through the sacrificial death of his Son. Counselling may well enable the client to accept themselves and feel good about themselves and this is no mean goal. Confession, however, says that I will not settle for accepting myself because I can only be really whole when I am forgiven by God and, hopefully, also by the one I have injured. This brings us to the experience of reconciliation.

(c) Reconciliation

We implore you on Christ's behalf: Be reconciled to God!
2 Corinthians 5:20

I once heard Grace Church, a missionary who worked in Brazil for the Overseas Missionary Fellowship, say that in trying to explain the meaning of reconciliation to the Amerindians she said it was rather like people being once again on speaking terms with each other. The meaning of the word *katallasso* is that of change or exchanging something. For the unsaved it could mean the change from no relationship with God to having a relationship; the change from being enemies to friends (Romans 5:10). It is the nature of God's saving grace that the door is opened so that we can confidently speak to him and he to us; such also is the nature of good friends. It must also be said that the scriptures do not teach that God himself needs to be reconciled to us; it is our need to be reconciled to him. This is supremely possible because it is God who has done something to provide a way or means of reconciliation. This is of course the atoning death of Jesus Christ upon the cross (Ephesians 2:16; Colossians 1:21). It is not the purpose of this book to explain the various theories and theologies of atonement which are available to us. Basically, the atonement deals with the 'how' of reconciliation through the cross. There seem to be three simple models which may be helpful to consider and reflect upon. The first is that of sacrifice: Jesus is the only offering by which our sins can be lifted. He is therefore the lamb who is killed for us to go free. The second is that of the slave market: here the model is that of paying the right price for our freedom. That price is the person of Jesus who in so doing finds the way to redeem, or buy back, that which had been sold. Finally there is the model of the law court; the sinner is justified although the charges of punishment have been passed. This is because we exchange roles with Jesus. He gives us his righteousness and agrees to take our sinfulness, and so receives the punishment which we deserve. An unfair exchange indeed, but it is the forgiven man or woman who sees the audacity of grace and nonetheless is glad to receive it. Paul says of this generous act, 'God made him sin for us, so that in him we might become the righteousness of God' (2 Corinthians 5:21). If you would like a more in-depth treatment of this subject then I recommend you read Emil Brunner's book *The Mediator*.[19]

Reconciliation is therefore a harbinger and testimony of spiritual renewal. It tells us that the old has passed away and that everything is becoming new. It also reveals how God not only loves us but respects our humanity enough to want to redeem us. It is a source of delight in God and in the gift of life itself. This is why Robin Green calls the sacrament of reconciliation the party for the world's liberation.[20] It is no coincidence that the Greek word from which we get our word 'eucharist', that ultimate sacrament of our redeemed status, means 'to celebrate', or 'to give thanks'.

(d) Restoration

I will restore the fortunes of Sodom . . . and your fortunes along with them.

Ezekiel 16:53

Dr Leslie Weatherhead, a Methodist minister and pioneer of

the relationship between Christian healing and psychology, gave a telling illustration of the meaning of restoration. He told of the story of Michaelangelo going down to the quarry to supervise the cutting of some marble for one of his sculptures. Whilst he was watching the men at work he suddenly shouted for them to stop immediately. He ran down and put his hands on a large piece of marble and said, 'Be careful how you cut for I can see King David in this rock and he is waiting for me to set him free.'

This speaks of how God sees how we have fallen and also sees how we can be freed to regain our full potential for growth. His work of salvation is then to rescue us from what binds and to restore us to our full personhood. It is a call to a relationship with God whereby the Holy Spirit not only is the agent of regeneration into new life but also the power for continuous renewal whose goal is to present us faultless before God in eternity.[21] Forgiveness may well be in a moment of realization, but restoration is a commitment to an eternity of growing in holiness. In fact, forgiveness leaves us no other choice.

To summarize, then, we can see how forgiveness restores our relationship with God and that from this all other healing relationships follow. Therefore to claim forgiveness from God but to sustain animosity towards another is actually to testify that I have not done anything with God's forgiveness except waste it. At the heart of forgiveness is a freedom to be creative about all the other dimensions of my life. The rest of this book will examine the implications of this more fully but suffice it for now to remind ourselves briefly of those dimensions.

2 FORGIVENESS AND MY RELATIONSHIP WITH MYSELF

Paul in writing to the Romans said, 'It is an agonising situation, and who on earth can set me free from the clutches of my own sinful nature? I thank God there is a way out through Jesus Christ our Lord' (Romans 7:25, J. B. Phillips' paraphrase). Forgiveness is a painful awakening on the one hand as we own our wrongdoings, but on the other it is releasing as we are given grace to accept ourselves with a new hope for change. This self-forgiveness does not mean absolving ourselves of the responsibilities and consequences of our actions but it emphasizes them all the more. 'It does not mean self-pity but accountability and repentance and change. It means facing the harsh realities of our actions and picking up our cross and following Jesus.'[22] I remember preaching on forgiveness in my local church in Leicester recently when afterwards a man came up to me and said that now he could go to prison with some hope in his heart. His court case had been pending and was about to come to a conclusion, but because he had been forgiven he could begin to come to terms with himself. He knew it wasn't going to be an easy future for him but he felt that he was only just beginning to learn to live with himself, something he had been running away from all his life. So often we do not like ourselves and forgiveness exposes this dysfunction in us and encourages us to walk in new life because if God can forgive and love us then we might learn to go and do likewise.

3 FORGIVENESS AND MY RELATIONSHIP WITH OTHERS

'By his stress on the necessity of a forgiving spirit Jesus . . . insists that repentance go beyond sorrow for sin and issue in a radical reorientation of the personality.'[23] It is incumbent upon the forgiven to be forgivers. Jesus points this out with his outrageous parable of the two debtors (Matthew 18:21–35). A king forgives his servant a million pounds but that self-same servant, upon discovering that a fellow servant who owed him a few pounds, could not pay his debt, has him dragged off and thrown into prison. Naturally when the king hears of this he has the first servant hauled before him and says to him, 'I cancelled all that debt of yours because you begged me to, shouldn't you have had mercy on your fellow-servant just as I had on you?' (18:32–3). And so the mean servant is thrown into the debtors' prison. Somehow, although he had been forgiven it did not change him into a forgiver. Our experience of forgiveness is also meant to act as a divine impulse to show us the healing property of forgiving, and impel us to go and do like-wise. To fail in this capacity is to negate the value of our forgiveness and ultimately drain it of any healing capacity for us or for others.

4 FORGIVENESS AND MY RELATIONSHIP WITH MY PAST

One of the reasons why some of us find it so hard to receive forgiveness is because we have been shaped and dominated by the damages of our pasts. God's salvation announces the heal-ing presence of Jesus not only in our today but also in our yesterdays. Paul speaks in Colossians of Jesus cancelling the past debts that hung over our lives so that we could go free from their power over us (Colossians 2:14–15). This is what is referred to by the healing of memories, where those scripts which we so often replay in our lives force us to live out that past routine in some continuous sense. When I worked with an evangelist with a real gift for coming alongside the homeless, he began to relive the feelings and the moments of former times when he was put into an orphanage. Although he was twenty-six years old he told me that when he was under pres-sure in some aspects of his work, he actually felt like that two-year-old boy. His feelings of guilt and worthlessness would surface and no amount of telling himself the theological truths of his new birth and acceptance in Jesus, which were in his mind, could convert his emotional map to the same reality. It was only when he learned to receive healing and forgiveness into his child memories that he found that the past no longer had a hold over him.

5 FORGIVENESS AND MY RELATIONSHIP WITH THE PRESENT

One of the hallmarks of forgiveness according to John Calvin was what he called 'vivication'. By this he meant seeing the reality of God's love so clearly that it produced an overwhelm-ing desire to live a holy life.[24] In other words, forgiveness is not just the removal of punishments upon a person but the infusion of a new will or desire to live for God in each present moment.

> Living in your presence Lord
> is life itself,
> I'm forgiven, I'm forgiven.
> With the past behind,
> grace for today
> and a hope to come.
> I'm forgiven, I'm forgiven.[25]

6 FORGIVENESS AND MY RELATIONSHIP WITH THE FUTURE

Donald Shriver writes of a meeting he once spoke at in an Episcopalian church in Atlanta, Georgia. In his sermon he referred to the official symbol of the city which was that of a phoenix rising out of the ashes. He said that as such it had shown that it had long recovered from the damages done in the Civil War when General Sherman had put much of the town to the torch. After the meeting a large majority of those well-educated, upper-class church goers said that all that he had preached was true except for the last part. They rejected wholly the suggestion that Sherman's sins against Atlanta could ever be forgiven.[26] Without forgiveness, therefore, no new future can be created as the past still moulds what is to come. We are consigned to repeat the past all over again until we have a fresh direction through forgiveness and inner transformation.

In conclusion, then, we can see the radical nature of God's salvation and forgiveness. If it be truly a work of grace it cannot and will not be contained within us. There is going to be an outflow of new life which will bring with it the healings which we need in order to grow into our full humanity. It is no small wonder therefore that Jesus impressed upon his disciples to be forgivers by the grace of the Spirit's power. We must not be like the Dead Sea which allows the fresh water of the river Jordan to flow into it but gives it no space to flow out. Consequently it is stagnant; you will not drown in it but neither will you find any life within it. If our forgiveness and salvation are to be of true value to us then we must be open to God to let this new life flow out and be shared in bringing life and healing to others.

Much suffering is caused by the fear of confessing and asking for forgiveness. I have seen the most radical changes in the life of people when they finally found the courage to confess what they felt most ashamed of or most guilty about. They discovered that instead of losing a friend, they gained one. Distances were bridged, walls came tumbling down and abysses were filled in.[27]

4

Forgiveness and Healing the Fellowship

If you don't have an environment of forgiveness you can't live freely. You can only defend yourself constantly.[1]

An offended brother is more unyielding than a fortified city, and disputes are like the barred gates of a citadel.
Proverbs 18:19

During the 1970s I took part in planning and presenting a Christian musical called *Come Together*, the score of which was written by Jimmy and Carol Owens. Under God it became one of the resources for renewal and evangelism for the whole of that decade. It was also the forerunner of enabling congregations to participate in praying with one another and so discover the value of shared ministries. As such it fostered interest in a number of celebratory style ministries which included the work of the late David Watson, as well as the enduring festival known as Spring Harvest. What I did not know was that the musical was actually a reflection of the story of a church in Van Nuys, Los Angeles.

Apparently this was a large Pentecostal church which had been decimated due to in-fightings and divisions between various families within the church. Consequently the congregation was reduced to a few handfuls. The church leadership decided to call a well-known and gifted preacher to be its pastor in order to help the church climb out of its rut and grow again. The man they invited was Jack Hayford, composer of such famous choruses as 'Majesty'. Jack came and subsequently accepted the invitation to the pastorate. However, as he was praying in the vestry prior to coming out to lead the worship he felt strongly impressed by the Lord that he was not to preach the sermon he had prepared; in fact he felt forbidden to preach at all. So he led the service and when it came to the place where he was to give his talk, he simply closed the service with prayer. Naturally there was the raising of some eyebrows and not a few questions were also raised. Imagine then how the congregation felt when this continued for several services!

Eventually someone came up and complained to him and out came what had been laid upon Jack's heart. He shared that he was well aware of the divisions within the church and that he did not feel that he could use his preaching to paper over the cracks. There first needed to be the healing of relationships if the fellowship was to grow and fulfil its calling by God. There was a stunned and embarrassed silence. Yet gradually one or two people began to share how wrong their attitude had been and slowly but surely the church began to find forgiveness and remove the obstacles to fellowship. It was in this way that the church began to 'come together' again. From this time of healing, that church steadily grew until it outgrew the building and a bigger one had to be built. It had fostered many missionary activities and much social enterprise within its own community. The church even changed its name to 'The Church on the Way', because it wanted to make the statement that there had been a time when it had been 'in the way' of God's purposes but, through forgiveness and healing, it was now on the way with God.

It was out of its experience of communal repentance and healing that the musical was written and so powerfully owned and used by God in American and Europe to bring restoration and renewal to an all too divided church. My involvement was largely based in Liverpool where it was thrilling and exciting to see Christians from both Catholic and non-Catholic churches working and witnessing side by side. It was the beginning of a spirit-inspired ecumenism which sought to proclaim Jesus as Lord rather than to alter or merge each other's structures of worship and practice. However, my own involvement came through a rude awakening rather than some cosy reflection.

At this time in my life I was a pastor of a very small pentecostal church which met in a school on a housing estate on Sundays and in the front room of our flat during the week. I was also a keen Protestant, which came largely through the church which nurtured me following my conversion to Christ and the Reformed doctrines which I believed then and, on the whole, still do. My convictions also came through the embittered feelings I held towards my father for the break-up of my family home which was nominally Roman Catholic. So my father's Catholicism became the convenient target for my hurt and angry feelings. It was into this situation that I was asked by a friend if I would like a good speaker to come to our mid-week Bible study. I readily agreed but only later learnt that the good speaker was Father Jerome McCarthy, a Benedictine priest born in the south of Ireland and currently working in a parish in Belfast.

I did not have the courage nor the honesty to cancel the arrangement I had inadvertently made with my friend, but hoped that Jerome would not be well enough to come and speak. However, he did come and as I delivered him to the door of our flat and ushered him inside I was surprised and nervous to see that a few religious sisters had also come along. Our small fellowship group seemed very nervous and confused about what was happening! This is understandable when you consider that there were quite a few others who held not only the doctrines but the attitudes towards Roman Catholics as I did. We quite arrogantly assumed that to belong to this particular denomination meant that you could not be saved!

Father Jerome must have guessed all this from the rather cold and nervous atmosphere which greeted his arrival. He therefore opened his talk with the colourful line, 'On the way to this meeting this evening, only God and I knew what I was going to say; but now only God knows because I don't have a clue!' With some collecting of his thoughts and feelings he simply shared his experience of being a parish priest in Belfast and how the Lord had challenged him to invite all comers to pray together in his church on Saturday night after the Mass was over. Eventually, Christians of all persuasions attended and they prayed for the peace and healing of Northern Ireland, and continued to do this despite interruptions and threats by the gunmen of both the IRA and the UVF. God's love triumphed over all obstacles and the Holy Spirit renewed their lives with grace and the gifts of the Spirit.

As I sat there listening to his testimony I began to think about my judgementalism and arrogance, of my bitter feelings towards my father and the intolerance I felt towards others. Basically, God's love and action in Jerome's life was exposing my wounded life-style. I was very thankful when another member of our church called Barry spoke up at the end and said, 'Brother, as I've been sitting here and listening to you, God has shown me how I have been judging others and I just want to say please forgive me.' He spoke the words I wanted to say. Jerome, with just a slight twist of humour, held out his right hand and whilst making the sign of the cross said, 'Well, I have been ordained to pronounce to people that their sins can be forgiven. So in the name of the Father, and the Son and the Holy Spirit, your sins are all gone!'

There was a brief moment of surprise after which we all suddenly burst into laughter; but it was a healing laughter as something very real was being exposed, forgiven and released by the Holy Spirit that day. For me it began a new chapter in my life which has been so important to me ever since. I still hold to the basic Reformed and Evangelical teachings I learnt at my conversion, but my attitude had been changed as my heart had been healed. From that day I have been involved in the whole Church of Jesus Christ and not just my own particular department. Soon afterwards I was invited to speak at a Roman Catholic charismatic prayer group in a convent in Birkenhead.

Since then it has been my privilege to have a share in the Holy Spirit's renewing work right across all the various Christian churches. It has been a great healing to my life and has taught me more about the reality and meaning of fellowship than perhaps anything else. What is more, the restoring of relationships with other Christians challenged me to heal the bitter root of hatred I held towards my father. He had remarried by now, and so I went and sought him out and asked him and his wife to forgive me for the way I had held such bitter feelings against them. I cannot say that the ending of that encounter was smooth or tremendous. My father was not quite sure how to respond, but we began to understand and accept each other from that day and over the years have grown to like one another. By the grace of God we still have room for improvement, but only so because I had first experienced the forgiveness which healed my fellowship with others and released me to see those areas where I could grow and develop.

From examples like this, therefore, we glean that fellowship is the vital resource from which we draw our inspiration, teaching, growth and support in our Christian life. If that fellowship is frustrated or hindered then we suffer the consequences. We are like a burning coal that has been taken out of the fire, we inevitably lose our flame and warmth. It is vitally important then that we understand the value and necessity of Christian fellowship and learn how to guard, protect and nurture it.

THE NATURE OF FELLOWSHIP

The word in the New Testament for fellowship is *koinonia* and is usually translated 'sharing in common', or 'communion'. As such it refers principally to the fact that as Christians, born again of the Holy Spirit, we share together in the life of Jesus Christ. Our common bond or place of communion is the life of Jesus Christ as continued amongst us through the active working of the Holy Spirit who has placed us 'in Christ'. It is a dynamic and not static fellowship. A. R. George says that the word and all its associates, of which there are forty-five examples, 'refer primarily to participation in something rather than to (just) association'.[2] It is not just the sharing of ideas or beliefs, but, foremost, it is the shared experience and awareness that Jesus is Lord amongst us and in the world. Therefore fellowship is a living, breathing reality. Like all relationships, it is kept alive and meaningful by continuous contact and mutual sharing through openness and love. It can also be ruined should we take it for granted and simply retreat from being engaged in meaningful interaction. We can also jeopardize our fellowship by keeping an unforgiving spirit towards those who are of our communion. The tragic reality is that because fellowship consists of two relationships, that between ourselves and God and also between each other, then should we fail in one, we fail in both.

John in his first Epistle links all these ideas together. He begins by underlining the relationship between believers: 'We proclaim what we have seen and heard, so that you also may have fellowship with us' (1 John 1:3). Here is the offer of sharing what has become real through encounter with Jesus Christ. Then John goes on to underline the fact that whatever is the reality of that fellowship between believers, their fellowship with the Father consists of exactly the same: 'And our fellowship is with the Father and with his Son, Jesus Christ' (1:4). The way the dynamic of fellowship works is first to establish what we share of Christ with each other and then to go on to have fellowship with the Father. Of course it has to be underlined that here we are speaking not of our individual walk with God, but with the true depth or shallowness of our fellowship as the Church.

I remember many years ago when I was the chairman of a Christian Union at Birkenhead Polytechnic and we were planning to engage in all sorts of evangelistic endeavours. However, there were serious disagreements between various members which had been left to fester. One of the older members of the Christian Union came up to me and challenged me about using evangelism as a means of avoiding healing the rifts in the fellowship. 'All we shall be doing', he said, 'is to invite people to come in and inherit the problems we already have. First heal yourself before proclaiming that others need saving.' His remarks were very powerful to us and the truth of the situation was all too clear. Therefore I cancelled the plans for outreach and invited each person to come to share in the breaking of bread together so that we might be healed of our differences. That time of prayer was the turning-point in our as yet small and intimidated band. One by one we confessed our sins to God and asked each one to forgive any wrong being held against them. Following on from this time there seemed to be a greater awareness of the presence of God and as a conse-quence more evangelistic enterprise with astonishing results.[3]

John went on to write in his letter, 'If we claim to have fellowship with him yet walk in darkness, we lie and do not live by the truth' (1:6). Before we confessed to one another our shared issues and problems we were not really walking in the truth together. Therefore it did not matter what amount of zealous enterprise we engaged in, there was a real sense in which it was not our truth. What is not truth, God will not bless. After all there is no fellowship between light and darkness (2 Corinthians 6:14). Confession brought us into the light with one another and there fellowship was restored (cf. 1 John 1:7).

THE NURTURE OF FELLOWSHIP

There is a whole chapter in the book of Leviticus which is largely devoted to what are called 'fellowship offerings'.[4] In fact they formed one of the five main temple sacrifices. The Hebrew words for fellowship offerings are *zebah shelamin*, and this is why they have also been called the 'peace-offerings'. The idea of peace in the Old Testament involves issues such as prosperity, bodily health, contentedness, good relations between men and nations, and also salvation. One of the Mes-sianic titles was Prince of Peace (Isaiah 9:6) and hence Paul picks up this theme and writes of Jesus coming to preach peace and to make peace between those whose fellowship had been broken (Ephesians 2:17). True *shalom*, therefore, 'is the gift of God, and can be received only in his presence'.[5] This is powerfully focused in the resurrection scene when Jesus appears to his disciples for the first time. Twice over he extends his shalom to them and links his offer of peace with his com-mission to evangelize and extend the ministry of forgiveness (John 21:19–23).

The fellowship offering is in many ways quite different from other Old Testament sacrifices in that it is essentially a com-munion meal. Here the meal is shared between the worshippers and the priests in the presence of God. As such it certainly prefigures the whole institution of the communion meal between Jesus and his disciples. There seem to be three reasons for this particular offering, those of thanksgiving, giving a vow of service (to God and the community) and a freewill offering. All of these are of course opportunities to nurture one's faith, but they are to be given within the context of a fellowship offering. Certainly, the New Testament equivalent of this passage could be that of Acts 2:34 which describes how the new Christians met together to 'devote themselves to the apostles' teaching and to the fellowship, to the breaking of bread and to prayer'. Once again fellowship is linked with a celebratory meal and personal growth. In conclusion, therefore, we can see that engagement in thanksgiving, works of service and personal growth is nurtured by the environment of fellowship. To be denied that environment, or to break it, is effectively to be damaged in all other areas. This is highlighted for me in the way that some church leaders have sought, perhaps too swiftly, to promote various ministries within a reluctant church and have run shipwreck on the rocks of opposition and, in some cases, have suffered personal breakdown. I think back to the time when I was an incumbent in a church in Leicestershire and inherited a healing service which was conducted each month during an evening Eucharist. No one came forward for prayer, and, despite my encouraging some people to give their testimony to healing and teaching on the subject, still no one came forward to receive prayer. As a matter of fact, attitudes hardened and the healing service became a bone of contention. After some prayer and consultation I decided to cancel this service. This was because it had become plain to me that we were a congregation without a fellowship and that it was the fellowship that needed attention rather than an aspect of ministry. Therefore I openly confessed to the congregation that I felt I was pursuing an issue of ministry when it was obvious that we were not one and for that I apologized. I then sought to attend to the need to restore a proper fellowship base and did in fact reintroduce the healing service later on and with much better support from the people and the encouragement of a number of healings from God.

Fellowship, then, is the context from which a number of partnerships and ministries develop and grow. These include evangelism and faith sharing (Philippians 1:5; 4:5; Philemon 6), growth in holiness (2 Peter 1:4), the renewal of the Holy Spirit (Philippians 2:1), encouraging and welcoming the ministry of others (Galatians 2:9), and ministry to the needs of the saints (2 Corinthians 8:3–4; 9:13). With such a potential for effective ministry, fellowship becomes a pearl of great price which must be guarded and fostered. There is a useful picture of this in the Septuagint version of Psalm 22 which says, 'Jerusalem is built as a city whose fellowship is complete' (verse 3). You get the picture that the city is secure and strong because its fellowship is intact. In fact this psalm links the ministry of *shalom* to the well-being of the city. There is the strength of tribal unity which is a testimony to the glory of God (verse 4), there are seats of leadership and judgement to the nation at large (verse 5), and there is economic prosperity which is good for the city as well as for the countryside (verse 8).

However, when this fellowship breaks down then the life goes out of our ministries. We may do the same things and say the same things, and God may even bring his blessing through it to others, but we do not benefit from it. Also the very thing that is meant to bring life becomes a focus for God's displeasure amongst us. A prime example of this is the abuse found amongst the Corinthians when they came together to celebrate the Lord's Supper, perhaps the most powerful symbol and sacrament of our fellowship together in Christ (1 Corinthians 10:16–17). Paul wrote to the church about their divisions and drew attention to the fact that their meetings did more harm than good (1 Corinthians 11:17). He underlines that because the fellowship was divided, they were eating the bread and drinking the cup unworthily and, as a result, some of their number were physically ill and some had died (11:30). This also illustrates for us the psychosomatic effects of spiritual, as well as emotional, dysfunctioning. Compare this with the account in John's Gospel where Jesus heals the man with long-term illness at Bethesda, and later forgives him his sins when he meets him in the temple (John 5:1–9, 14). We are not told what his sins were but we are shown that his physical condition was in some way a product of his sinfulness. Therefore Jesus says to the man, 'Stop sinning or something worse may happen to you' (5:14). The Corinthian church had devalued the meaning of fellowship and as such they were paying a bitter price for their neglect. Hans Küng, in affirming the importance of the communion, does in fact underline the importance of remaining in fellowship with each other;

> The Lord's Supper is the centre of the church and of its various acts of worship. Here the church is truly itself . . . here the church of Christ is gathered for its most intimate fellowship, as sharers in a meal. In this fellowship they draw strength for their service in the world. Because this meal is a meal of covenant and fellowship, the church is essentially a community which loves without ceasing. Essentially, therefore, the church must be a meal fellowship, a *koinonia* or *communio*; it must be a fellowship with Christ and with Christians, or it is not the church of Christ.[6]

So we can see that some of the effects of broken fellowship were both spiritual and physical. The remedy was not to pray for healing but to restore fellowship. When Paul gives instructions to put things right his first priority is consideration of each other so that fellowship is renewed and healing will follow as a consequence. Doubtless, an essential ingredient in the process is forgiveness. Such restoration is not easy and can be very demanding. 'The process of making revisions is painful, sometimes excruciatingly painful.'[7] I well remember attending the International Charismatic Conference on World Evangelisation in July 1991 at the Brighton Centre. On the Thursday evening the main speaker was Father Raniero Cantalamessa, a Franciscan Capuchin who was also a Papal preacher to the Pontifical household. Before giving his address on the Holy Spirit and Evangelism, he first declared that he was unable to speak until he had received forgiveness from the five thousand delegates who were there. He believed that there needed to be a proper acknowledgement and release of the past animosities and divisions between his church and other non-Catholic churches. It was a powerful and moving admission of our need for healing. It was also a great risk in honesty and humility as in the audience were bishops and an archbishop of his own church. I thought it all the more powerful considering that all week the conference had been picketed by certain groups who objected to the erroneous teachings of the Roman Catholic delegates who were attending and taking part. If only they could have listened to this godly man expound the scriptures so effectively and evangelistically. Father Raniero's words were first greeted with total silence as the implication of what he had said struck home. Although it is only my own intuitive awareness, I did feel that I and many thousands more were echoing his words and also acknowledging the need to see healing and restoration within and across the churches. He then went on to pray his prayer of repentance which was genuine and entirely devoid of theatricals because the Holy Spirit used it to address a real wound we were all feeling. In that moment I really did feel that we had come to the brink of an enormously important opportunity on God's agenda. I am sure that we were being presented with a *kairos*, something of God's timing for the release from the effects of centuries of divisions and bitter warfare. It was a prophetic encounter through which we heard God saying, 'This is my word to you, hear it and take it to heart.'

At the end of the talk, there was thunderous applause that went on for almost five minutes. It signalled a cry from the heart for restoration and forgiveness, which has always been one of God's priorities for his people. People all over the auditorium began to turn to each other and offer the sign of peace. For others it was a mixture of tears and joy as old enmities and new forgivenesses were realized. I thought of the exhortation and call to prayer which God gave to Israel when it had prepared a temple fit for his worship:

If my people, who are called by my name, will humble themselves and pray and seek my face and turn from their wicked ways, then will I hear from heaven and will forgive their sin and heal their land. (2 Chronicles 7:14)

It was in the healing of relationships which that night of confession and forgiveness brought that I saw the great potential for effective evangelism in the power of the Holy Spirit. We cannot hope to heal a world's broken relationship with God if the proclaimers themselves are not healed in their own relationships. Of course, this is not to deny that there may well be a need for doctrinal reform, but surely the basis for this comes from establishing that we do indeed have fellowship through our Lord Jesus Christ. This is in fact the rebuke that is given to the Ephesian church by the exalted Jesus. They had established a reputation for doctrinal excellence and purity but they were commanded to repent because they had forsaken their first love (Revelation 2:1–5). Their first love was surely to love God with all their heart and soul, and their neighbours as themselves. It is often said that this is the eleventh commandment for Christians as John specially writes about it so much: 'A new command I give you: Love one another. As I have loved you, so you must love one another' (John 13:34).[8]

Surely, then, in this decade of Evangelism, we should also address the healing that is needed in our own home. There are of course some new initiatives already taking place in this country which deserve our support and prayers. Two in particular that have encouraged me recently are the joint evangelistic missions being conducted by Fr Pat Lynch of the Sion Community and the evangelist Revd Eric Delve of the Down to Earth Trust; and also that between J. John of the Philo Trust and Father Ian Petit, a Benedictine monk based at the St Bede's Centre in York. Ecumenical evangelism in the power of the Spirit is, I am sure, going to be a feature of God's restoring and renewing work in our world.

We have been examining how fellowship is important for the nurturing of our personal growth as well as the ministries entrusted to the Church by God. Let us go on then and look at what we need to do in order to enable our fellowship to be the healed resource we so vitally need.

THE NEEDS OF FELLOWSHIP

Of course here we could just quote the statement attributed to Augustine which says, 'love God and do as you like', meaning that if we learn to love the Father properly all other priorities and needs will be automatically met and fulfilled. There is indeed a truth at the heart of this, but the matter is both as simple as this and also more complex than this. Love needs to be directed and worked out in action and there are three actions I wish to focus upon in particular.

1 Unity

> *How good and pleasant it is when brothers dwell together*
> *in unity . . . for there the Lord bestows his blessing.*
>   Psalm 133:1,3

The Apostle Paul had no doubt witnessed the breakdown of a number of churches which he had worked hard to establish. It comes as no surprise therefore that when Paul comes to reflect and write his later letters he includes the importance of Christian unity. I am referring of course to his Letter to the Ephesians. The whole book is a continuous reminder of our oneness both in Christ and subsequently with each other. There are a number of graphic images presented throughout the book which represent the church in its internal relationships, and they all convey the essential cohesive and indivisible reality of those relationships both with Jesus and with its members. It is this unity which makes its fellowship and ministry so vibrant and powerful. They are those of the head and the body (1:22–3; 2:16;4:12,16;5:22–33); the bridegroom and the bride (5:25–32) and the cornerstone and the building (2:19–22).[9]

Standing at the heart of his letter is his great plea that the church be united under the power of the Holy Spirit: 'Make every effort to keep the unity of the Spirit in the bond of peace' (4:3). The interesting thing to notice is that we already have unity and so it is not a cry to go and make unity but to go out and keep it intact. There is a great difference between the two. Only the Holy Spirit can make us one by bringing us to peace in Jesus through his blood shed for our sins. If unity is lost it is because we have broken it and need to return in penitence and cry for the Spirit to breathe upon us once again and recreate a new unity. Paul goes on to offer a number of ways in which we work to maintain unity but he first joins this quest with that of holiness. 'Be completely humble and gentle, be patient, bearing with one another in love' (4:2). This is not to be a cold academic pursuit of unity but a holy endeavour, because the stakes are very high, namely the presence of a living Church which will shine its gospel light within the dark skies of our world. I think of the prayer of Jesus in the garden of Gethsemane when he had the relationships of his friends very much on his heart. It is recorded that he prayed for their unity three times and each time coupled it with the need for the world to know the gospel through the quality of life of the Church. He prayed, 'May they be brought to complete unity to let the world know that you sent me and have loved them even as you have loved me' (John 17:23; cf. John 17:11, 21).

Unfortunately, holiness has not been a subject of great interest within our churches and consequently standards of Christian living have been eroded in the process.

> This relative eclipse of holiness as a main evangelical concern is little short of tragic, and I hope it will not long continue, particularly in a day of such striking evangelical advance in numbers, in institutional resources, in mission strategy, in academic achievement, in public standing, and in many other respects. We need to be clear in our minds that none of these advances are going to count for much in the long run unless renewal in holiness accompanies them.[10]

Let us now look at the ways in which Paul encourages the Ephesians to maintain their unity.

(a) By remembering our common life in Jesus (Ephesians 4:4–6)

Everything that Paul lists here makes the Church what it is, the body of Christ. If we are not one here then we are not the Church. I have often been thankful when I have been sharply reminded of the fact that a person I may dislike or disagree with, but who is nonetheless a Christian, is just as much a part of the one faith, hope and body of Christ as I am. When I was a pastor in Birkenhead I found that I just could not get on with another member of the church who disagreed with just about everything I said and did. (Incidentally, he was often right!) He was forceful and very capable and gifted and was convinced that he should be pastor instead of me. I think that this may well have been at a time when I was unsure about my future. It came to a stage where I couldn't speak with him without boiling over inside. I would come home to my wife, Carole, and immediately begin to pour out my hurt feelings and disgruntlement with him. Sleep became a difficulty and I discovered one day that I had mouth ulcers. I had to do something to break the destructive cycle going on in my heart.

Then one day someone said to me, 'You know, he loves God just as much as you and, what is more, God loves him just the same as you!' It was an obvious and simple truth but it challenged me deeply. I suddenly realized that in nursing my grievances against him I was not only destroying the unity which the Holy Spirit had given to us but I was in reality denying him the same hope, the same Lord, the same faith, the same baptism and the same, one, membership of the body of Christ. I now found that I could pray for him with good intent and in time with real warmth. I asked God to give the biggest blessing he was capable of containing, and every time I was tempted to indulge in my heated feelings I reminded myself that we shared one body, one Spirit and the one God and Father of us both. In time, not overnight, we both learnt to recognize and accept our differing styles as well as giftings. Today we are good friends but we have always been one in Christ Jesus.

Similarly Paul lists what we share as God's loving and saving gift of grace and he fully intends this to be an incentive to maintain that unity which is God's gift to us at salvation.

(b) Shared grace and charismatic gifts (Ephesians 4:7–11)
Another way to work at strengthening our unity is to recognize and acknowledge the workings of God's grace and gifts amongst us. Jesus was always swift to recognize grace in others and was not afraid to say so. When the Roman centurion confessed to Jesus both his unworthiness for him to come into his house and his knowledge of Jesus's authority to speak words of healing, Jesus said that he had not seen such faith anywhere in Israel before (Matthew 8:8–10). It is our calling to go and do likewise, to recognize God's grace in others when we see it. I am sure that we need to recover the ministry of encouragement within the Church. We need a few more people like Barnabas (called 'son of encouragement') who can come alongside those whose gifts are not recognized and affirm them and release their giftings for the benefit of us all. Where would the Apostle Paul have been without the insightful care of Barnabas? Probably he would have finished his days as the semi-ostracized man of the desert he was when Barnabas went and found him and brought him into belonging.

Paul couples the picture of grace and gifts with the imagery of conquest. He takes the words of Psalm 68:18 which actually says of this conqueror that he 'received gifts from men', and changes the words to 'and gave gifts to men'. He is showing that Christ is indeed a conqueror who has gone up on high into the heavens, but instead of taking booty from those he has defeated, his victory releases the gifts of the Spirit for the building up of the Church. The grace gifts therefore are a reminder of what God has won and brought together and their use is to further that victory. This is clearly the case in the Acts of the Apostles as in demonstrated by the unifying power of the gift of speaking in tongues. On the day of Pentecost we are told that people from a variety of regions across Asia heard the praises of God spoken in the language of their adopted homeland; remember they could all speak Aramaic no doubt (Acts 2:7–12). On that day they were united in hearing God's praises. A second example is that of the experience in Cornelius's house. When Peter had to report back to the church in Jerusalem and authenticate the conversion of the Gentiles, he referred to the fact that they had received the Holy Spirit in the same way as the apostles, with the accompanying manifestation of tongues and prophecy. This is what convinced the apostles that the Gentiles had also been granted the gift of salvation (Acts 11:17–18).

Perhaps we should also underline that the gifts of God are not our possession or even profession. By this I mean that they are not given for us to keep and compare what we may have, but they are given in order to be given away. They are, after all, grace gifts and so by definition they are to be an offering of grace for others. I remember many years ago listening to one of the pioneers of charismatic renewal, David Du Plessis, in the Free Trade Hall in Manchester. He challenged us all by saying that the gifts of the Spirit have not been given to us. Then he paused to allow us to absorb what he was saying before he completed his sentence by saying they are given through us! He illustrated this by saying that if we should be invited to pray for someone's healing, and after such prayer that person was healed, which one would have the gift of healing? The one who prayed or the one who was healed? The answer is, of course, the one who was healed. The gifts of the Holy Spirit are given through us to others; they are for the common good (1 Corinthians 12:7). Incidentally, the only exception to this rule is possibly that of speaking in tongues, as its principal function seems to be that of a private prayer language (1 Corinthians 14:2–4).

Paul specifically lists what are called ministry or functional gifts within the Church; they are apostles, prophets, evangelists, pastors and teachers. Whatever their order may signify, they are all a reminder that God takes some people and makes them gifts to the Church, and as such they should be received and respected. The right honouring of such gifts and grace in us all is what helps to keep our unity meaningful and functional.

(c) By releasing and fulfilling the work of God's Kingdom
(Ephesians 4:12–16)

Paul has his eyes firmly on the goals which God sets for this expression of unity. It is not self-indulgent but is quite practical in that it results in everyone finding their appropriate service to others (4:12). However, even this is not the final goal, for all our ministries are to enable us to attain the whole measure of the fulness of Christ (4:13). Frustrate that unity, then, and the works of service are stifled and the growth of the Church is stunted. I was once struck by a preacher who used a stark image to depict the church that had lost its unity. He said that such a body of Christ is as painful and difficult as a spastic body which, despite the clear commands from the person inside, does not respond properly. The signals from the head keep failing to reach the other parts of the body and so it just doesn't respond. Our glorious head is Jesus, but so often the body has been racked by disunity and has become almost dysfunctional.

The remarkable lesson from these verses is that it is not just the ministries of those listed that effect this goal, it is everyone's ministry. So whether we be a prophet, gifted with healing, a great evangelist or someone with charismatic gifts of help (1 Corinthians 12:28), they all form the network through which God is at work to bring us to complete unity and maturity in Jesus Christ (Ephesians 4:12–13, 16). I have already mentioned the time when I was the pastor of a Pentecostal church in Birkenhead. What I did not mention was that we met on Sunday mornings in the staff room of the local middle school. The room always smelt of stale cigarettes and drink and it took some time to forget about the smells before the worship could be properly enjoyed. One of our fellowship was a researcher at a local chemical plant and he decided that he would come in earlier one Sunday and clean and polish the room before the meeting. The change was immediate. Instead of feeling depressed about the atmosphere and finding it hard to pray, the clean and bright room beckoned us to worship! I considered it to be a powerful gift to our fellowship and growth.

I suppose one of the key clauses in these verses is the end of verse 16: 'as each part [person] does its work'. Here is a strong incentive to promote and guard this unity we have been given in Christ; if I damage our oneness then I limit your service. If I limit your service to me and others then we cannot attain to that full stature of Christ because neither of us has been fulfilling our calling aright. Therefore God calls us to 'dynamic interaction'.[11] I cannot sit passively by and watch that unity wither because it affects my own growth as a member of the body of Christ. This is one sickness which we have all been called to heal.

2   Discipline

Wounds from a friend can be trusted, but an enemy multiplies kisses.

Proverbs 27:6

William Barclay once complained that the Church of Scotland was failing to grow in holiness because there was a noticeable absence of discipline reported at the annual conference. Discipline can be understood in two basic ways: the correction of wrong behaviour such as withholding privileges from a child because it has done something it knows to be wrong; and the routines of control we use in order to achieve a particular goal, such as an athlete training in order to be fit for his race. Without discipline, we invite lawlessness in the first example or unfitness or unreadiness in the second. The New Testament employs both concepts of discipline to describe the growth of the Church. The basic word used is *paideuo* which primarily denotes the training of children. The idea is one of instructing in right behaviour, so the emphasis is less upon punishment and more upon restoration. 'Brothers, if a man is caught in a sin, you who are spiritual should restore him gently' (Galatians 6:1). Yet we must not imagine that such discipline is soft or non-confrontative. The writer to the Hebrews uses the same word in conjunction with rebuke and punishment (Hebrews 12:6–7). Consider how strongly Paul commands the church to remove from its fellowship those who flout the moral code of holiness (1 Corinthians 5:1–5).[12] There is also the detailed procedure outlined by Jesus to restore a brother who has sinned against you or to remove him if he refuses correction (Matthew 18:15–19). It should be noted that the context for these disciplines is that of binding or loosing, of discovering what is forgiven and what cannot be forgiven because there has been no restoration.

There came a time when I had to remove someone from a church I once pastored. It concerned one of the leaders who had had an affair with a married woman. At the time he thought nothing was wrong despite the many discussions we shared. This happened at a time when the church had dwindled to a congregation of about nine and, needless to say, I was reluctant to remove this man for fear of the effect it might have on the few who remained. They had had enough pain through various disputes by which a number of people had already left the church. I prayed quite a lot and my course of action was patently clear to me from Scripture. I felt very depressed and weak at this time but I sent for him and told him that I had to stop him from sharing in the communion and, because he was unrepentant, also to remove him from the church. It was all the harder because he had been with me from the beginning of the church and had worked very hard indeed to see it established. The following Sunday I informed the church and in accordance with the biblical instructions we prayed for his restoration. I then quoted the words from Corinthians that we should 'hand this man over to Satan, so that the sinful nature might be destroyed and his spirit saved on the day of the Lord' (1 Corinthians 5:5).

Wilmington points out that the word for destruction here means to spoil or mar and therefore refers to the person being spoiled in their practice of sin in the hope that they repent and return to the Lord.[13] Far from our fellowship being demoralized by the diminishing of our numbers, they actually felt relieved and that God was affirming the importance of the church through such actions. Needless to say we earnestly prayed for our friend to come to his senses and return to us. Our prayers were answered in dramatic fashion as he came to my flat a few days later seeking forgiveness and repentance because he now saw the full impact of what he had been doing. In time he was restored to the full communion of the church and continued to serve it with renewed vigour and love. The fellowship also respected him a lot for the disciplines he had accepted in order to be properly corrected before sharing in the communion again. Discipline had been seen to be done and it affirmed for that little congregation that their holiness and spirituality were important. It also challenged us all to pay greater attention to our need for support and guidance in growth.

The other word used regarding discipline is *sophronismos* and means soundness of mind. When Paul wrote to the young pastor Timothy, in order to strengthen his resolve to be a witness, he wrote, 'For God did not give us a spirit of fear, but a spirit of power and love and a sound mind' (2 Timothy 1:7, J. B. Phillips). This second form of discipline is a personal routine of a holy and anointed life which each person commits themselves to. No one else can make us do it or even monitor what we do. Yet the results can be seen in the quality or otherwise of the fellowship. When John wrote his third Epistle he referred to a member of the church called Diotrephes who seemed to be ambitious and who would not respect the ministry or leadership of the apostle (verse 9). John announces in his letter that when he next comes to them, he will confront him about it (verse 10). When the fellowship of the church is suffering, the causes for it need to be confronted, not ignored in the hope that the situation will improve. We must also be careful not to substitute forgiveness for confrontation. I know of a number of churches which have been plagued with certain divisions for some considerable time and various people have encouraged everyone to forgive each other and be reconciled. This is of course very commendable and right, but those churches are still in difficulties because there has been no acknowledgement of the actual issues and problems which have torn them apart. Discipline is to be a holy confrontation in which those who do the confronting first consider their own lives and take care to exercise their authority in humility and love. The ultimate aim is restoration where forgiveness can not only be given but properly received.

3   Forgiveness and the Christian day of atonement

Do not hold against us the sins of the fathers; may your mercy come quickly to meet us, for we are in desperate need.

Psalm 79:8

Some fellowships need healing from their pasts. Because these issues have not been properly dealt with their effects linger on in the lives of the next generation. After all, what has not yet been forgiven is not yet released or healed. This is surely the motivation behind some of the great prayers in the Bible. Consider the prayer of Daniel where he identifies the sins of Israel as his own and asks God to free his captive people from the consequences of those sinful actions (Daniel 9:4–19). He reminds himself that the result of such rebellion against God is that the people, both near and far, have inherited both shame and the curses of disobedience mentioned in the book of Deuteronomy (Daniel 9:7–11; cf. Deuteronomy 28:15–68). The nation in captivity is really the prisoner of a former generation's sins:

O Lord, in keeping with all your righteous acts, turn away your anger and your wrath from Jerusalem, your city, your holy hill. Our sins and the iniquities of our fathers have made Jerusalem and your people an object of scorn to all those around us. (Daniel 9:16)

In order for healing and deliverance in the present, there was need for the past sins and issues to be cleansed. Daniel calls for a precise response from God; he wants the Lord first to listen to his confession, then to forgive, and then to act in healing and deliverance (9:19). We should not be surprised therefore if we find that our churches struggle or feel trapped by the unfinished business of their own past. Part of the healing which God wants to bring is to churches as a whole, as well as to individuals. For some years now I have been engaged in working alongside whole congregations to teach and enable them to find release from this kind of past agenda in order that they may be released to be the people of power which God has called them to be.

My involvement began when I was approached by a group of Deacons from a Baptist church who had a growing concern about the health of the new pastor and his family. This family had moved into the city some three years earlier and since then there had not been a time in their experience when someone was not ill in some way. They had been prayed over, deliverance prayers had been offered, they had all had a medical check-up to see if they were carrying any viral illnesses; in all departments there was no result or response to give any clue as to why they had so much illness. However, one of the leaders pointed out that the chapel had a history of schisms and splits and, consequently, the ministers who came did not stay very long. The latest row concerned a minister of some years earlier who had sought to introduce charismatic renewal into the church in a rather tactless way.

The more I prayed and reflected on the situation the more my mind came to these prayers of Daniel and of Ezra before him who located the problem of the present with the unhealed sins of the past. In studying further I began to see that one of the greatest needs in our churches was healing from the false ministries of those who had gone before. Somehow we need to be freed from the legacies of the past and especially those who occupied the place of ministry or leadership. It was after all the sins of the leaders of the people for which God was punishing the whole nation. Forgiveness was the key ministry which was needed whereby God would release those who were captive to the consequences of other peoples' sins as well as their own. Doubtless this may also be coupled with other needs, such as deliverance ministry, which will be discussed in more depth in a later chapter.

In reply to Daniel's great prayer the angel Gabriel said that seventy years of captivity must first pass in order to put an end to the nation's sins, to atone for their wickedness and to bring in the righteousness of God (9:24). It is the ministry of forgiveness and atonement that I want to pay particular attention to. The word atonement in the Old Testament is *kippur* and basically can mean 'to cover, to pacify or to ransom'. William Gesenius said that it also means 'to be delivered from the effects of'. This comes from the fact that the word is also used for the 'wiping the face clean which has been blackened by displeasure'.[14] In the New Testament the equivalent word is *katalage* and basically means 'to be reconciled'. As part of their spiritual discipline, the Israelites were instructed to have an annual day of atonement. What intrigued me was examining the actual historical reason for its institution; it was the breakdown of ministry, and consequently the people needed to be set free from the effects of this.

'The Lord spoke to Moses after the death of the two sons of Aaron who died when they approached the Lord' (Leviticus 16:1). The two sons in question were Nadab and Abihu who had fallen dead before God because they had taken upon themselves an unauthorized ministry. They had obviously been caught with the idea of basking in the power and the glory which they saw accompanying Moses' ministry in the tabernacle. So they went through exactly the same motions as Moses, but their hearts were full of pride and they paid the price (cf. Leviticus 9:23–10:3; Numbers 3:2–4) It seems that that rebellion now prevented Aaron from conducting his ministry as freely as before. However, the effects of their unauthorized ministry were felt not only in their father's ministry (Leviticus 16:2), but also in the very building itself. There was to be atonement first for the minister and his household (16:6, 11), then atonement for the most holy place especially, as well as the whole of the tent of meeting (16:16). There is to be cleansing for the altar (16:20), and then in conclusion, atonement for the whole community (16:19, 24, 29–30). It is clear from this that the day of atonement was not only a response to a particular need to release and renew minister and congregation alike, but also as a resource for continuous healing and forgiveness within the whole community on future occasions.

I suddenly realized that here was an actual process by which forgiveness and release was brought to a whole community as well as release to the place of ministry and worship from the effects of anything spiritually unclean. Why can't we follow a similar procedure? I do not wish for a moment to undermine the once for all, sufficient sacrifice of Jesus Christ upon the cross for the sins of the whole world. I do, however, wish to apply its power in every legitimate way possible. This was when I suggested to the Baptist church that they had a Christian day of atonement (see Appendix 2). By this I mean that just as the Old Testament community assembled before its building and confession and atonement were properly offered for the ministry conducted there, for the sins of the people and for the cleansing and healing of the building, we should do likewise in the name of our sinless high priest, Jesus Christ.

Therefore a day was arranged when the entire congregation was invited and informed of the purpose of the meeting which was to seek forgiveness and healing from anything from the past or present which was keeping the church in bondage. People were asked to come in not to watch but to be prepared to confess their own sins either verbally or by writing them on pieces of paper. The papers would later be burnt but not read. There was to be no blaming of individuals from the past, but the present leadership would, like Daniel and Ezra, ask the Lord to forgive the sins of their forebears as well as their own. There were to be prayers in the pulpit, at the communion table and indeed at all the significant places where ministry was conducted. These prayers were for cleansing from any of the ill-effects which may be associated with them. Appropriate space was given for sharing the peace or finding reconciliation with people in the church itself. It was a great moment of healing for that fellowship. The pastor and his family, whilst experiencing the usuals ups and downs of coughs and colds, never again were inflicted with constant ill-health within the family. The church was also enabled to pick up the experience of spiritual renewal and leave behind the frictions and animosities caused by its earlier presentation. As a result of this Christian day of atonement, the Lord had indeed brought healing to the church on a number of levels. This was precisely the intention of the original *yom kippur* and as Christians we would do well to learn some of these lessons from the Old Testament and not sweep them away because our focus is now on what the Lord Jesus has done for us on Calvary. Christ has indeed made atonement for all our sins but I think we need to reclaim something of the process by which this full salvation can be applied to the body of Christ today.

As Christians, therefore, we have been called into a community committed to forgiveness within and then from the fellowship. 'By doing the will of God we shall belong to the covenant of forgiveness.'[15] Luther said that forgiveness is that experience which allows the Holy Spirit to return to us and enliven us again.[16] The Church must not allow itself to be like Samson whose fellowship had long been broken but who nonetheless went out to battle thinking everything was the same as before: 'But he did not know that the Lord had left him' (Judges 16:20). He went through the familiar motions of renewal but there was no power there anymore and he was badly mauled in the process. So we must keep our fellowship alive and whole through the ministry of forgiveness. If we will be the anointed people of God who will take the healing presence of Jesus Christ into a world that has long been fragmented and lost its place of belonging, then we must first be a healed family.

5

Forgiveness and Personal Healing

You should get into the habit of admitting your sins to each other, and praying for each other, so that if sickness comes to you you may be healed.

James 5:16 (J. B. Phillips' paraphrase)

I suppose one of the most remarkable demonstrations that forgiveness brings physical healing is the story of the paralytic who was lowered through the roof of a house by his four friends (Mark 2:12). It is a graphic scene which Mark paints; the preacher's sermon is interrupted as remnants of the roof are showered on the congregation below, then silently the paralytic is lowered to the feet of Jesus who looks up and reads all the hopes and fears and faith that was in the faces of the four friends. The sick man does not say a word; he is helpless but present. He offers no explanation of his problem and does not ask for healing either; that request has been spoken in the actions of his friends.

Jesus, having looked up at the four friends, now looks down at the man before him and says, 'Son, your sins are forgiven' (2:5). I think that it is significant that the first word Jesus spoke was 'son'. The word here is *teknon*, and Lawrence Richards says that the term is used to denote the special relationship between a child and its parents or family.[1] This same word carries theological importance because it is used to describe believers as the children of God and therefore as co-heirs with Christ (John 1:12; Romans 8:16–17).

It is, then, a term of endearment that Jesus offers to this stranger and as such reveals a number of things. It tells us that

Jesus is fully aware of this man's emotional state and need; it also tells us that Jesus is able to meet this man at the point of his need. Jesus is telling him that he belongs, that he has a place in someone's family, the family of God. It is significant after all that it is his friends who so determinedly bring him for healing and that no mention is made of his family in this enterprise. I am quite sure that it is the word of sonship which awakens the man's heart to receiving forgiveness for his sins. This illustrates for us that Jesus is not cheaply offering forgiveness, there is awareness and timing in what he says. He is careful to awaken the son to being a son before he restores him to his heavenly Father's forgiveness. It tells us that before we can receive the forgiveness of sins we so much need, we must first be brought to the place of recognition and ability to receive it and take it to heart. The very word from which the name of Jesus originates means 'to be spacious',[2] and illustrates the way in which Jesus is always offering us healing space where he can be made alive to our need and find grace to help in time for that need.

Jesus' first words to the paralytic also reveal to us that the most important healing needed was not physical but spiritual. However, he did not leave it there as he also went on to heal his paralysis. It is not actually stated that the man's physical illness was due to his sin, but the process of healing which Jesus adopts suggests that this was indeed the case. However, it needs to be pointed out here that not every illness is due to sin as Jesus himself stated in the case of the man who was born blind (John 9:3). The healing of the paralytic also reveals that God is committed to healing the whole person, body, soul and spirit. The healing also presents us with a reminder of the general order of ministry for healing the whole person: first comes the proclamation of the good news, 'your sins are forgiven'; then follows the sign of wonder of healing, 'Get up, take your mat and go home'. In all the commissions of ministry this is the pattern which is adopted.[3] Even the prayer of the emerging and persecuted church follows this process: 'Grant to thy servants to speak thy word with all boldness, while thou stretchest out thy hand to heal, and signs and wonders are performed through the name of they holy servant Jesus' (Acts 4:29–30, RSV).

Forgiveness became, then, not only the means of his spiritual healing but also the enabling gift to effect physical healing. Why is this? First we need to understand the fact that our physical condition is sometimes related to our emotional and spiritual well-being, or ill-being as the case may be.

FORGIVENESS AND HEALING THE WHOLE PERSON

In Psalm 38 King David writes about how his many illnesses are as a result of his sins and the guilt which he carried.

> O Lord, do not rebuke me in your anger
> or discipline me in your wrath.
> For your arrows have pierced me,
> and your hand has come upon me.
> Because of your wrath there is no health in my body;
> my bones have no soundness because of my sin . . .
> My wounds fester and are loathsome
> because of my sinful folly.
> I am bowed down and brought very low;
> all day long I go about mourning.
> My back is filled with pain;
> there is no health in my body.
> I am feeble and utterly crushed;
> I groan in anguish of heart . . .
> My heart pounds, my strength fails me;
> even the light has gone from my eyes.
> My friends and companions avoid me because of my
>   wounds;
> my neighbours stay far away. (Psalm 38:1–11)[4]

David's condition is one of festering sores, a general breakdown in physical health and energy, and alienation from God. All equally prey upon his mind. His condition resembles that of Job, although the latter's problems were not as a result of his sin but as a consequence of spiritual warfare. Some commentators suggest that the context for this penitential psalm are the two grievous sins of adultery with Bathsheba and the engineering of the murder of her husband, Uriah.[5] In verse 3 the word for health is *shalom* and so the verse could just as easily be translated, 'There is no wholeness (soundness) in my body.' The psalmist is acknowledging his physical illnesses, but he is also exclaiming his need for repentance and forgiveness if he is going to be healed. That great Evangelical preacher of the nineteenth century, Charles Spurgeon, wrote:

> Mental depression tells upon the bodily frame; it is enough to create and foster every disease, and is in itself the most painful of all diseases. Soul sickness tells upon the entire frame; it weakens the body, and then bodily weariness reacts upon the mind . . . Deeper still the malady penetrates, till the bones, the more solid parts of the system, are affected. No soundness and no rest are two sad deficiencies; yet these are both consciously gone from every awakened conscience until Jesus gives relief.[6]

This sounds so modern a view and underlines for us the growing conviction within psychosomatic medicine that there is a very real connection between physical health and emotional health.[7] Matthew Linn writes: 'In the past we didn't think anger and guilt could trigger any physical illness besides an occasional headache or possibly an ulcer. Thus we always attributed the cause of heart disease primarily to the misuse of cholesterol or cigarette smoking and cancer to carcinogenic particles.'[8] However, due to the work of researchers like Dr Meyer Friedman and Dr Carl Simonton, the connection between unresolved guilt and anger and the role they play in triggering and maintaining some heart diseases and cancers has been widely established.[9] Recent studies carried out by Manchester University's Department of Psychiatry and the Institute of Psychiatry in London have confirmed that between a fifth and a third of all patients who go to their GPs with a physical symptom have no detectable physical illness. They have observed a growing opinion amongst senior hospital doctors that many of their patients' illnesses have a more subtle basis. Dr David Goldberg,

Professor of Psychiatry at Withington Hospital in Manchester, has coined the term 'somatiser' to describe these patients whose physical pains and problems originate with their emotional stresses and strains. He maintains that although many doctors dismiss psychosomatic pains as imaginary and incurable, the pain experienced can be greater than that suffered by patients with organic disease.[10] In the opinion of the researchers it was felt that a revolution in medical care was needed so that due attention was paid to the need to heal the often torn and fragmented world of a patient's emotions because the unhealed feelings held the body, to some degree, within a parallel orbit of illness. Dr Chris Bass, once a GP but now a consultant psychiatrist and lecturer at Oxford University, said that this preoccupation with the body not only wasted an enormous amount of resources – estimated at a minimum of one million pounds each year in hospital time and resources – it could also have catastrophic effects upon the patient:

> Many hard core chronic somatisers end up having operations they don't need. In a recent survey of 33 such patients at King's College Hospital in London, two-thirds had under-gone at least one major surgical operation in the absence of any clear evidence of disease. More than half of the women had had hysterectomies.[11]

So it is apparent that, for some people, the route to healing for their bodies is not that of surgical medication but the healing of their emotional ills and sins. This is in fact the model which Jesus gives in the healing of the paralysed man.

Charles Williams says that the healing in that home offered strange things to the questioning congregation. The strange things were the 'double renovation of power', the power to forgive sins and the power to heal the body.[12] For Jesus, whole-ness, and not merely curing, was his chief goal in his healing ministry. This is also illustrated in the healing of the man at the pool of Bethesda who was described as a long-term disabled man (John 5:3–5). At first glance this may seem to be a reverse of the paralytic's story because Jesus heals his body and only later on, when he meets him in the temple, refers to his sinful life which had resulted in his disability (John 5:14). However, it is surely implicit in Jesus' approach that he extended forgiveness in his healing encounter because the man is found afterwards in the temple, presumably there to give thanks and worship. Also when Jesus confronts him he does not raise the issue of forgiveness but a continuation of his renewed life-style. This is surely to suggest that forgiveness was in the gift of healing and no doubt enabled the man to be open to healing as he seemed to be vague about his needs when asked if he wanted to be well (John 5:6–8).

Rita Bennett, although speaking of inner healing, offers a useful way of understanding the forgiveness healing which the paralysed man received: 'The first forgiving is on the level of your relationship with God. The second forgiving is on the level of your relationship with others. The first cleanses you in your relationship to God. The second releases you in your relationship with people.'[13] The first forgiveness restored the paralytic to his place of belonging; he first belonged to his heavenly Father and was restored to his spiritual family. The second forgiveness took the form of healing his body and then redirecting his steps towards his relationship with his family. According to the Markan version of the story, Jesus commands the man to 'get up, take your mat and go home!' (Mark 2:11).

In my book *Healing Dreams* I mention a time when I went to see my mother about something that had been on my mind for some years. At the time I visited her she was living on her own having divorced my father some years earlier. I talked about my feelings and then I asked her to forgive me for holding deep-seated grudges against her for many years. I wasn't really prepared for what happened next. My mother told me that I was the first person in her whole life who had asked forgiveness of her. She then told me all about her life and childhood. Her mother had died when she was three, and so she was raised by her half-sister who had an affair with her father. She had been beaten as a child and had felt lonely all her life. She married my father during the early years of the War and there had been many difficulties which resulted in an affair and the birth of a daughter. Apparently my father came home on compassionate leave and gave my mother the choice of saving the marriage by giving up her daughter or keeping her daughter but ending the marriage and losing the son they had had between them. She gave away her baby girl, but had felt guilty all these years and, thirty-five years later, she still longed to see her daughter again. 'Can God forgive me?' she asked. I told her that if God could forgive me my sins he could surely forgive her sins too. So she asked me to pray with her and I had the joy of leading my mother to a true faith in Jesus and the knowledge that her sins were forgiven. My mother started living in the real world and we found that she could relate normally for the first time with adults. She found a new freedom with the rest of her children, and so was able to share with them her secret and, perhaps for the first time in her life, feel accepted by those she loved.[14] A few days after this meeting my mother telephoned me to say that she had found it difficult to sleep during the last few days. It transpired that she no longer needed to place a huge wooden door underneath her mattress to support her bad back which she had had for over twenty years. Neither did she need to wear a support for her back and, with her doctor's supervision, she also gave up taking her pain-killing tablets as she no longer needed them. She had been healed of back ache.

David Seamands mentions a magazine article which was called 'Confession may be good for the Body'.[15] It went on to say:

New studies show persuasively that people who are able to confide in others about their troubled feelings or some traumatic event, rather than bear the turmoil in silence, are less vulnerable to disease . . . Dr James Pennbaker's research shows that the act of confiding in someone else protects the body against damaging internal stresses that are the penalty for carrying around an onerous emotional burden such as unspoken remorse. Similar research conducted at Harvard University shows that those who do not share have less effective immune systems.

So we can see that because we are a unison of spirit, soul and body, forgiveness becomes a divine chain reaction which

does not stop at spiritual issues only but opens up the possibilit-
ies for the presence of the healing Christ to enter the whole of
our person.

FORGIVENESS DISARMS THE POWER OF INTERNAL BLOCKAGES TO HEALING

There are times when we cannot be healed because we are too
focused upon our own wounds. We are not open to receive the
word of life even when it is offered. This is what lies at the
heart of the Emmaus road journey. Cleopas and his friend are
walking away from Jerusalem on the third day, and they are
deep into discussion about all the events that had happened.
However, Jesus joins them, but they cannot see who he is and
so when he asks them what they are so animatedly discussing
they challenge him by saying, 'Are you only a visitor to Jerusalem and do not know the things that have happened there in
these days?' (Luke 24:18). What irony! After all, Jesus is the
only one who does know. Yet he does not burst out with an
ill-timed revelation but he asks them to explain what they mean
and then patiently lets them tell their story, the heart of which
contains the great hurt, 'We had hoped that he was the one
who was going to redeem Israel' (24:21).

This is an important lesson in the healing of hurts and the
removal of the inner blindness and blockages we all carry. Jesus
employs two basic ministries here, that of listening and that of
the rightly-timed word. He could so easily have revealed himself to them but it was important to give them space to get out
what was locked within and then bring the word, because only
then could it be properly heard and responded to. It is important to note that the true servant of God, according to Isaiah,
is someone who will know the time and the place to offer the
word which brings life to the needy:

> The Sovereign Lord has given me an instructed tongue
> to know *the* word that sustains the weary.
> He wakens me morning by morning, wakens my ear to

listen like one being taught. (Isaiah 50:4, my italics)

It was Dame Cicely Saunders, founder of the hospice move-ment, who said that 'someone will say more in a climate of listening'. How true this is; sometimes the route to forgiveness and healing is not the challenge to see the truth, change direc-tion and repent; it is finding the place where I can speak out all the issues which clog up my life even if they are distorted and hard. That place is in the presence of the listening Christ and his representatives. Like Job, who all through his so-called counselling sessions with his four friends, having poured out his hot and bitter feelings as well as his sense of indignation about what had happened to him, realized he had been doing so in the presence of God and then, and only then, found more space to repent of his wrong words (Job 42:3–6). It is important that the words and feelings are known to be heard by another because this is a healing facility which enables a person to identify such feelings and then let them go and move on with their life. I remember listening to a person who wished to talk about the difficulties they were experiencing both with depression and with their Christian walk. At one point in the conversation the person mentioned a relative's death which had happened almost a year earlier. 'I've got over that now', she said. I simply reflected back her own words with the same weight and emphasis she herself had used. However, in hearing her own words coming back to her she could listen for the first time, at depth, to what she had actually said and wanted to say. There was a period of silence as she allowed herself to take to heart what she really meant and then came the tears. She had not got over the death and what is more, the subject still very much affected other relationships within her life. Eventually she realized that she had not really been facing up to the implications of all this and that this was why she had found it so hard to move forward in her life. It was in being given space to say her own words and weigh them which offered her the moment of insight and the opportunity to let go and forgive herself and others. There is in fact a whole ministry of listening which is a skill which more and more Christians are becoming aware that they do not possess and wish to learn.[16]

Listening is not only the context for forgiveness; it is to offer space in which forgiveness can take place. It is in fact a forgiving act in itself because it invites both confession and redirection. What has not been truly heard cannot be properly forgiven. The two on the Emmaus road confessed their beliefs and their broken hopes, and it was into this that Jesus spoke the burning words which enabled them to repent, to change direction and move forward in faith. St Teresa of Avila calls this encounter that of the true contemplative which always results in true forgiveness.[17] Cleopas and his friend were enabled to offer confession in the presence of Jesus because he listened, and once this was done they were in a better place to hear the word of God for their lives. The Roman Catholic practice of the confessional works on this very principle whereby we are given room to confess whilst another holds our words with a true listening heart. Then follows the gift of God's word of forgiveness followed by the word of direction and possible restitution. It must not be assumed of course that listening is a totally passive affair in which the listener merely absorbs the words of the speaker like blotting paper soaking up some spilt ink. Listening, like forgiveness, offers a frank and honest sharing of the relevant issues, otherwise the whole encounter is meaningless and the circumstances of our lives remain unchanged.

A good summary of the process of listening and the way it leads to forgiveness, and consequently healing, are the words of the psalmist when he cries:

> See my sorrows,
> feel my pain,
> forgive my sins.
> (Psalm 25:18, Living Bible paraphrase)

Good listening also challenges us to face up to and own our areas of denial. The walkers on the Emmaus road were actually in possession of all the facts about Jesus, including the testimony of both the women and Peter and John that Jesus had risen. Yet they could not really take to heart the obvious

implications of what they had been told because their ability
to understand was blocked by the deep hurt of their broken
hope (Luke 24:21–4). So often our denials are not so much a
lack of knowledge but a refusal to 'own' that knowledge
because we are nursing a greater wound of some kind. Robert
Bly calls denial a form of amnesia.[18] He is thinking especially
of the effect of traumatic experiences upon a child whereby the
little boy or girl is entranced by that past encounter and as such
brings into adulthood an ocean of oblivion which attempts to
block out the feelings of shame or pain. However, the wall of
our denial is often breached in our dreams or through some
later event which triggers the memory and we relive the pain
and the emotions of those former times as if they were happening now, and to some degree we become our child again.

> Something in us prevents us from remembering, when
> remembering proves to be too difficult or painful. We forget
> benefits . . . we forget former loves . . . we forget our former
> hates . . . we forget former pain . . . we forget guilt. We
> repress what we cannot stand. We forget it by entombing it
> within us. Ordinary forgetting liberates us from innumerable
> small things in a natural process. Forgetting by repression
> does not liberate us, but seems to cut us off from what makes
> us suffer. We are not entirely successful however, because
> the memory is buried within us, and influences every moment
> of our growth. And sometimes it breaks through the prison
> and strikes at us directly and painfully.[19]

Forgiveness offers us the space to see our wound and lay it
at the feet of Jesus, and as a result we are enabled to see the
whole story which concerns us. Matthew and Dennis Linn
write: 'The main thing that Christ seems to say when I am in
denial is, "Don't be afraid but share with me whatever is hard
to face." '[20] As Jesus began to open the scriptures to Cleopas
and his friend he was in effect taking them back down memory
lane, but this time from his perspective. It was this that gave
them the fuller picture of their circumstances and brought healing to their memories. Forgiveness, therefore, is also a ministry
of listening which helps a person to confess their needs and

hurts as well as own what they have denied. This removes those internal blockages and so allows our faith to reach out to the Christ before us and receive the healing that he offers.

FORGIVENESS OPENS THE DOOR TO THE PRAYER OF FAITH

A reason why there may not be healing is often because the offer of healing is not met with faith in the recipient. Forgiveness often helps us to regain our lost faith. Once the two friends on the road were open to hearing the word of Christ their faith was renewed. Later they reflected on that moment and said, 'Were not our hearts burning within us while he talked with us on the road and opened the scriptures to us?' (Luke 24:32). And having received such words they were now in a better place for their faith to come alive again. They recognized him! Sitting down at the meal table, Jesus broke the bread in his usual manner and prayed, and in the offer of sharing they could see who he was. What was present to them all the time, they were now able to recognize because Christ's forgiving presence had renewed their faith and faith can see where feelings cannot. Suddenly they were running back to Jerusalem to add their words of faith and vision to that of the other disciples.

I think of the message of the women who burst into the upper room on the resurrection morning to announce that Jesus was alive. They carried the instructions of angels who said, 'Go, tell his disciples and Peter' (Mark 15:7). Only the Markan account makes the personal reference to Peter for whom this little statement would have been loaded with tremendous implications. It meant that the Jesus who had died had understood the bitter tears he had shed before that charcoal fire when he had denied he ever knew Jesus (Luke 22:61–2). It also meant that the risen Jesus had forgiven him and expected to meet him as still one of the disciples' band in Galilee. Perhaps this explains the enthusiasm with which Peter joined John in rushing to the tomb to see the Lord for himself. Only the forgiven run so openly to find their saviour. The 'and Peter' element of the angels' message told Peter that he was a forgiven man; his faith was suddenly released and, like an arrow shot from a bow, he runs to the tomb in the hope of meeting Jesus for himself. It is the same impulse of the forgiven with faith which finds him jumping into the lake and wading to the shore to be with Christ. Interestingly enough, when he gets there, he is confronted by a charcoal fire. This word, *anthrakia*, occurs only twice in the New Testament and they both concern Peter's statements about Jesus.[21] I am quite sure that Peter immediately connected the fire on the shore with the one in the High Priest's courtyard. However, this time he is given space to declare his love for the Lord and makes that so poignant comment, 'Lord, you know all things, you know that I love you' (John 21:17). The 'all things' no doubt included the former fireside denunciations. Yet he can confess this to Jesus because he knows that he is forgiven. This is affirmed when Jesus takes Peter back to his original calling and reminds him that his commission is still in place; he said, 'Follow me!' (John 21:19).

Forgiveness therefore is a rescue work which delivers us from the confines and consequences of our own actions and opens up the future by removing any internal blockages we may have and releasing faith into action. The words of the psalmist who had been delivered from the stranglehold of his enemies seems appropriate here: 'He brought me out into a spacious place; he rescued me because he delighted in me' (Psalm 18:19; 31:8). The Septuagint word used here for spacious (*platuno*) is also used in the New Testament for the 'enlargement of the heart'. It refers to the freeing and deepening of fellowship between brothers who open their lives in care for each other.[22]

For Peter, then, his forgiveness set him upon a journey to free him from his past actions and choices. Jesus offered him another opportunity to affirm his love for God, whereas before he had denied him. Therefore the fire on the shore was a focus through which he could journey backwards to that other fire in the courtyard and, by the grace and power of God, undo the effects of that former moment. Derek Prince identifies three elements to Peter's restoration by the fire: repent, revoke and replace.[23] The repentance, however, is already revealed in the fact that Peter was in that upper room with the disciples waiting and wondering about what God was going to do next. He is quite correct when he says that for Peter to be healed of the effects of his denial, which amounted to putting a curse upon himself (Mark 14:71), he needed to replace his former wrong confession with a right one. This model of forgiveness and healing in the life of Peter introduces us to the whole area of ministry known as healing of the memories, and to this we shall now turn our attention in the next chapter.

6

Forgiveness and Healing of Memories

God, grant me the serenity
to accept the things I cannot change,
the courage to change the things I can,
and the wisdom to know the difference.
Living one day at a time,
enjoying one moment at a time,
accepting hardship as a pathway to peace;
taking, as Jesus did,
this sinful world as it is,
not as I would have it,
trusting that You will make all things right
if I surrender to Your will;
so that I may be reasonably happy in this life
and supremely happy with You forever in the next. Amen.
Reinhold Niebuhr, 'The Serenity Prayer'

WHAT IS HEALING OF THE MEMORIES?

Before going any further we need to clarify what is meant by healing of memories, for not everyone is happy with the various practices that are associated with it and dispute whether it is really Christian. I believe that the term was first used by Agnes Sanford and referred to focusing the healing power of Jesus on the memories and moments from a person's past which still exerted some form of control or shaping upon their present behaviour. At the heart of the ministry is a form of prayer ministry by which the individual is encouraged to relive certain hurting memories, into which the healing presence of Jesus is invited in order to bring about the desired healing and change of living for the future. Selwyn Hughes, a Christian counsellor and writer, says that the term is not found in the New Testament and that it is more closely related to psychoanalysis and psychotherapy than Christian ministry.[1] He goes on to point out that inner healing is more concerned with change and relief than growth into the likeness of Jesus Christ. I find he presents an unnecessary and to some degree artificial polarity in his argument, as surely those who find relief and change are now in an even better place to experience the Holy Spirit's transforming power in their lives.

David Seamands, on the other hand, reminds us that remembering is central to the biblical tradition of spirituality.[2] At the heart of the Eucharist or Lord's Supper, stands the request by Jesus that this sacred meal be done in remembrance of him (1 Corinthians 11:25). It demonstrates that remembering is the bringing forward into the present of an event from the past, not in a mere mental act but to some degree re-experiencing what that past event still has power to deliver. Consider, for example, the fact that there is a whole book in the Old Testament which is devoted to the subject of memories! This is the book of Deuteronomy which comes from the Greek word meaning 'a second time' and whose key word is 'remember'.[3] Throughout the book readers are encouraged to remember the former days and how God had judged and delivered them from their enemies. The clear indication of the book is that they were to learn the ways of God from what they remembered and make sure that they did not repeat the mistakes of the past, but choose a better pathway for the future. Naturally such memories would evoke both facts and feelings which in themselves would exert some sort of power and influence in the life of the individual. Therefore the ministry of healing the memories would similarly deal with bringing under Christ's rule the emotions and issues of the past which still threaten to destroy our growth and wholeness in Christ. This is surely suggested by the passage in Jeremiah 31:34 which says, 'I will forgive their wickedness and will remember their sins no more.' The text is found in a section dealing with the new covenant to come which was fulfilled in the person and work of Jesus Christ. It links the ministry of forgiveness with that of putting aside or removing the power of past moments over a people. Perhaps we need to underline that it does not mean that God forgets, but rather that he chooses not to remember those memories that he has forgiven. Therefore they exert no more threat or power over the lives of the forgiven. Here is God healing memories both for himself and for us.

In working with memories there is of course a need for care and caution before proceeding. We must be sure that the individual is ready to look backwards and willing to confront and take responsibility for what may be found there. There are two equal and opposite dangers which we must avoid, that of denying the importance of the feelings and issues shared in this work and that of relying solely upon reliving the past event in order to bring healing and relief. Once I received a telephone call from someone in distress after being prayed with for such a healing. She complained that the hurtful memory had not gone away and she could still remember the event she wished to forget and be free of. Apparently she had been told that she did not need to understand her memory but be delivered from having it! So we need to declare clearly that healing of the memories is not an attempt to anaesthetize our remembering but at least to understand how our past experiences are to some degree still exerting an unhealthy influence upon our present conduct. Then comes the opportunity to challenge and change our response to that past memory. This can only happen when we accept our responsibility, not for the event which concerns us, but for the choices we made in the past and can choose to change in the present. John White seeks to present a balanced view of working with memories when he writes:

> From childhood, we are responsible for our actions and our attitudes, even those that arise from misconceptions and mistreatment. I mention this because some people pursue what is called healing of memories or inner healing . . . the idea is that the recovery of the memory, along with some comforting association (such as a mental picture of Jesus) will produce

healing. Yet unless the moral aspects of the problem – which include the response of the person doing the remembering – are faced, the experience is unlikely to lead to permanent change.[4]

He goes on to write that we can pursue this form of healing in vain unless there is an understanding that although we cannot be responsible for the things that have happened to us, we must be responsible for the way we have responded to those things. It is this step of accountability which is actually the threshold of healing because by the grace of God we can be changed from being the prisoner of our pasts and choose a new response through the power of the Holy Spirit within us. An example of this is what happened to a mother in Norwich Cathedral on Mothering Sunday. She had come with her husband to take part in a healing service which I was conducting. After some teaching, I encouraged those who wished to to turn to a partner for a healing prayer which took the form of a silent prayer. I then encouraged everyone to be still and listen for the voice of God speaking into their hearts and making them aware of the particular need he wished to bring into contact with his healing presence. When they knew what this need was, they were to squeeze the hand of their prayer partner who would pray a simple, one-sentence prayer such as 'The healing power of the Lord Jesus Christ meet you at your point of need'.

The lady in question was reluctant at first to join in the exercise, even though provision had been made for people to sit quietly and pray on their own should they not wish to share with a partner. The reason for this was because she and her husband had not really prayed together for about fourteen years, since their daughter had tragically died of an illness. However, they held each other's hands and both silently offered the same grief of the loss of their little girl. The grieving mother became aware of how she had held bitterness against God for this death and that she had not really let go of her daughter's death and gone forward in her own personal growth as a Christian. In their time of prayer, they both confessed this fact and so the tears began to flow as the woman also accepted God's love and so forgave herself for holding on to so many hurting feelings. It was at this moment that she also realized there was a little girl inside herself who had been dominated by her mother in childhood and, just as her mother would not let her go, so she would not let her dead little girl go. She saw that she had allowed her mother to go on dominating her life and that she needed to be forgiven not only for letting her but also for complaining down the years that she did so. She told me that in stopping the nursing of her grief for her little girl, she had suddenly been offered a chance to grow up and put away her own childish things. Threaded through the whole prayer experience had been the grace of God forgiving her her sins and setting her free from the power of hurting moments. The journey of healing therefore is not so much to relive or re-experience the past but to gain insight as to how those moments still exercise an unhealthy hold over us today; to appreciate the way in which our choices reinforce their grip upon us; and finally, with the help of Jesus, to renounce this old order of slavery to our woundedness and to choose the pathway of new life in Jesus Christ.

> The therapy that heals these deep wounds could be called the forgiveness of sins, or it could be called the healing of the memories. Whatever one calls it, there are in many of us wounds so deep that only the mediation of someone else to whom we may bear our grief can heal us.[5]

That mediator is of course our Lord Jesus Christ. Unhealed wounds from the past function rather like an emotional and spiritual stronghold within our lives. Let us briefly survey some of these strongholds and see how the way to freedom is so often the way of forgiveness.

THE STRONGHOLDS OF UNHEALED MEMORIES

> *The very weapons we use are not those of human warfare but powerful in God's warfare for the destruction of . . . strongholds. Our battle is to bring down every deceptive*

fantasy and every imposing defence that men erect against the true knowledge of God. We even fight to capture every thought until it acknowledges the authority of Christ.
2 Corinthians 10:4–5 (J. B. Phillips' paraphrase)

The above passage is first and foremost dealing with spiritual warfare in a general sense and is painting the conflict of oppositions to the rule of Christ which the Christian has to confront. However, it is also an apt description of the inner battle to be engaged in when we need to be set free from the stronghold of unhealed memories. Interestingly enough there are three strongholds mentioned and they all have something to do with the power of words: they are arguments, pretensions and thoughts. The implication is that as Christians we sometimes hold fast to ideas and beliefs which we may not actually believe. The Apostle Paul refers to this very fact when he cries desperately:

My own behaviour baffles me. For I find myself not doing what I really want to do but doing what I really loathe . . . I often find that I have the will to do good, but not the power . . . I observe an entirely different principle at work in my nature. This is in continual conflict with my conscious attitude and makes me an unwilling prisoner to the law of sin and death . . . It is an agonising situation, and who on earth can set me free from the clutches of my own sinful nature? I thank God there is a way our through Jesus Christ our Lord. (Romans 7:15–25, Phillips)

Unfortunately we are held fast by the way certain hurtful or damaging actions and words go on speaking to us with precisely the same effect as they did when first encountered. David Benner says that an alarmingly large percentage of all children hear repeated verbal put-downs from adults who are not able to recall their own childhood reactions to such emotional insults. Comments such as, 'You are going to turn out to be as worthless as your father', or 'You idiot, you haven't got a brain in your head!' wound us long after we stop showing any reaction to them. They shape our self-image and often function as self-fulfilling prophecies, producing the very effects they were intended to discourage.[6] These words act like personal scripts which we live out, much to our own disapproval, and they need to be appropriately located, challenged and replaced with the words of God's truth about our lives and person. We can only guess what scripts were circulating in Job's mind when, in his time of suffering, he cried out, 'What I feared has come upon me; what I dreaded has happened to me' (Job 3:25).

We must not underestimate the importance or power of words in our lives. The very creation itself was brought into being by the words of God. God said, 'Let there be' and there was. This same creation is held together by the word of God's command (2 Peter 3:5, 7; Hebrews 1:3; 11:3). So often we are told in the Old Testament that the word of the Lord came to the prophets who made known the mind and actions of God to a people too preoccupied to hear the word for themselves. Indeed the prophet is anxious to point out that no matter what others may say, the word of the Lord will not only endure forever, but it will ultimately achieve its purpose (Isaiah 40:8; 55:11). Jesus is revealed as the divine Word which was in the beginning with God and who will return as judge of all people (John 1:1; Revelation 19:13). The power of words is also revealed in the sad tale of Esau coming to his father Isaac for the blessing due to the first born, only to find that his younger brother Jacob had deceitfully stolen his blessing. Esau, however, assumed that once the fraud had been uncovered his father would simply repeat the words of blessing over him and he would inherit his due blessings from God. What a shock it must have been to hear his father saying that the words once spoken could not be changed or immediately retrieved (Genesis 27:30–8). The words once spoken would have a due effect and they could not simply be unspoken. So it is with us, our memories often speak with the same effect the words or actions which caused us pain. Therefore we need to take heed of the teachings of James when he writes about the power of the tongue to hurt or heal a person. He reminds us that the tongue can be an instrument to bless or to curse (James 3:5–10).

Derek Prince develops this argument when he says that the self-fulfilling prophecies we carry act rather like self-pronouncing curses in our lives. He begins by pointing out that the main vehicle for both blessings and curses is 'words'.[7] This is illustrated by the following texts from Proverbs:

> Reckless words pierce like a sword,
> but the tongue of the wise brings healing.
> (Proverbs 12:18)

> The tongue has the power of life and death,
> and those who love it will eat its fruit.
> (Proverbs 18:21)

Derek Prince then goes on to mention how idle words will be judged by Jesus (cf. Matthew 12:36–7) and that to some degree they take root and affect our lives even if we did not consciously mean them. He quotes the example of Jack who said to his wife, 'I'm sick of the way you serve our meals.' Apparently, the result of this kind of statement was that 'he brought upon himself the curse of indigestion that continued to afflict him for the rest of his life'.[8] However, I think that Derek Prince overstates the case here because the words of Jesus are spoken in the context of blasphemy against the Holy Spirit and the words that come from an evil heart and a good heart. At the day of judgement our response to the Holy Spirit will be examined and judged. It is perhaps more accurate to say that Jack's indigestion was a result of the attitude to life that was in his heart, and that it was from this condition that he spoke, rather than his words causing his condition. Yet this is not to undermine the care we need to exercise with our use of words, not principally for the effect they may have upon ourselves, but upon them to whom they are spoken. Derek Prince's book *Blessing or Curse* does develop another aspect of our subject which is worth exploring, and that is the generational effects of curses and of how there are times when the memories which need healing are not actually our own but those of former generations. Quite often we find people living out life-styles and associated fears which do not correspond to their own experiences, but are in fact the handed down scenarios and effects of their ancestors' experiences.[9] The family problem can be of the type mentioned in Exodus 20 where the consequences of the sins of the fathers are passed down to the third generation (Exodus 20:4–5) and which are presumably broken by the repentance of family members on behalf of their forebears. Other times it is that the children have imbibed and inherited their parents' ways of reacting to life situations and have passed their own responses down to their children after them even when the former prevailing situations no longer exist.

So far we have explored the way in which some of our memories still have the power to hurt us, and hinder us in our growth in grace and the true knowledge of God through our Lord Jesus Christ. We have seen that at the heart of such memories there may be certain words or actions which continue to shape our present-day activities and responses.

The power to hurt us so profoundly usually comes from various authority figures such as our parents or teachers or ministers. Most counsellors say that the time of hurting is usually within childhood when the infant is so dependent upon another for protection, nurture and affirmation. Robert Bly describes the implanting of bad moments or memories as those times when the parents ignore the child's sense of sovereignty and simply invade their sense of privacy.[10] So when the child looks for safety and is sexually abused, he or she loses their sense of worth and feels worthless and full of shame. Very often such feelings in the child are accompanied by a conviction that it is their fault that such things happened and this results in a guilt that is very difficult to find forgiveness for precisely because it is false guilt. What follows is a sense of being unprotected which can result in withdrawal from full commitment to others for fear of being invaded again. So much of the healing needed in our world today is for the adult person to seek out and find their little inner boy and girl and bring to them the love and protection they may not have been afforded earlier. Once the little child in us is healed then the adult can get on with their life!

Some years ago I went to a friend to have some counsel

about feelings of sadness which I had carried around within me for most of my life. I could not think of anything traumatic which had happened to give rise to such feelings. There was no tragic death within the family and no memories of being harshly treated by my parents or teachers at school. As I began to talk I suddenly had a picture flash through my mind of myself at the age of seven years. I was standing in a park with a football and had no one to play with. This was quite strange as I am one of five children and never wanted for playmates at any time in my youth. As I looked at this inner picture those old familiar feelings of sadness began to surface. So much so that my counsellor, observing how sad I was now looking, asked me how I was feeling. My eyes filled up with tears and I blurted out, 'I want my Daddy to play with me!' With the words, my tears turned into sobs and I had a good cry. Somehow the crying helped me to gain clarity in my thinking. I realized that all through my childhood, I and my brothers and sisters had lots of love from our mother, but no such encounters with our father. He lived in the same house but hardly spent any time with us and when we approached him to play with us he would tell us to go away because he was too tired. Nothing very dramatic you would say, but I saw that I had concluded that I was not worthy to be played with and so never asked anyone to help me because I felt that I would be refused once again. My mind told me that I had lots of friends but my feelings were those of the little boy who felt rejected and worthless. My father, I should point out, is not an ogre; he did not know how to play because his father had never played with him either. The counsellor helped me to see that inside me was that little boy still waiting for father to come out and play. I needed to recognize how I had responded to those days now long gone and how I was still choosing to retreat, and so repent and change my attitude and be more open to others. It was a real help to be encouraged to speak to that child part of my make-up and tell him that I loved him and, what is more, that the Lord Jesus did as well.

Before exploring some of the ways in which we bring forgiveness and healing to painful memories, let us look at some of the indicators that reveal a need for such a healing within us and some of the ways in which we are able to locate the point of pain itself.

SOME INDICATIONS FOR THE HEALING OF MEMORIES

Traumas which are repressed will inevitably be repeated until they are remembered.

Sigmund Freud[11]

1   Denial

The first line of defence against emotional pain is often denial. It is our attempt to say that some experiences simply did not happen. This phenomenon is well known in such things as bereavement because we are not able to accept the implications of what has happened or to cope with the feelings of loss and pain. This is why the some people report seeing their deceased relative sitting in his or her favourite chair or doing some of the things they usually did such as read a paper or smoke a pipe. Elizabeth Kübler Ross, in her research concerning the feelings of the dying and the bereaved, identified denial as the first stage in this process of coming to terms with a death. The other stages are anger, bargaining, depression and acceptance.[12] She stresses that we go through this process at different speeds and that we are each different and must not try to rush through so that we end up with a cheap healing. It is important, therefore, for those in denial to first work through any feelings involved before coming to the place of healing.

Denial is also directed towards feelings and experiences which threaten or challenge the way we conceive of ourselves. For example, many Christians believe that they should not be depressed or that they should not fail because through Jesus they should be able to have the victory over every event. When things do go wrong and they cannot find a reason for it nor learn a lesson from it, they pretend that all is well. There is the fear that they must have sinned in some way for these things to be happening to them. So they simply eradicate such feelings from their conscious awareness. However, such feelings still continue to exert an influence within their lives and often result in breakdown at some point.

I remember talking with a middle-aged woman who came forward at a Eucharist for prayer with the laying on of hands. She was overweight and wanted help to slim down to something more reasonable. As I listened to her she displayed a good knowledge of dieting procedures and had tried them all. She had managed to stick to the routines prescribed but had not seen a satisfactory weight loss. Before praying we asked the Holy Spirit to make her aware of any other area in her life which needed God's healing presence and which would help her to control her weight. After a few minutes of silence she began to share a particular memory which went all the way back to when she was a little girl in Chester. She remembered sitting in a high chair and being fed by her father. Suddenly her mother appeared in the room with her suitcase packed. Apparently she announced that she was finally leaving home and, turning to the girl in the chair, said, 'And you can keep that fat ugly baby, I never want to see her again!' With this her mother stormed out of the house and the woman had never seen her ever again. The moment of recall was actually quite upsetting for this lady because she began to share how she had grown up hating her mother, as well as the aunt who actually brought her up, until she too left home in order to get married. Her hatred of her mother was bound to her mother's words of calling her fat and ugly. When she realized this she asked God to forgive her for hating and renounced her mother's opinion of her. We met some years later in a prayer meeting when she loudly announced that she had lost quite a bit of weight even though she had a very good appetite. It seems that her inability to lose weight was connected to her lack of ability to free herself from her mother's parting rejection. She had transferred the hurt of her mother's words to the size of her body; it was a way of displacing her feelings.

There are other ways of engaging in denial; often we try to shut the hurting feelings away deep inside. The trouble with this is that we are in danger of blocking off all our other emotions so that to others we seem cold and unfeeling. However, it is our way of defending ourselves from being hurt again. An extreme form of this is that known as 'multiple personality', whereby an individual constructs a number of alternative *personae* who each deal with the unpleasant aspects of their journey through life to date. The central core of the personality disowns these memories and the feelings associated with them. This is often what is happening to those who have endured long-term sexual or ritual sexual abuse. Each *alter* or *persona* handles a separate part of the story of the individual's life; sometimes there may be no awareness or contact between these different personalities. The work of healing is to bring awareness, integration and healing between the various *alters* and the main core of individual awareness. In one sense such a situation, though complex, is really a testimony to the ingenuity of the person to create such a structure and survive with some sense of purpose and function in life. Perhaps we need to mention at this point that there is a time when denial is quite helpful for coping in the short term with experiences which are overwhelming, such as bereavement or some other form of shock. However, if it continues to shield us from, rather than prepare us for, reality, then denial has become a work of distorting our perceptions and needs to be appropriately confronted.

2 Determined to be different

So often we find ourselves saying that we are going to do things very differently from the way they were done to us when we were children. For example, it might be never spanking your children because you were spanked too much as a child; or never drinking alcohol because your parents were always drunk; or compulsively buying new things because you are haunted by the memory of the poverty you grew up in. Dave Carder calls this the 'reaction formation'.[13] It is a form of disassociation by which we try and tell ourselves that certain uncomfortable feelings do not belong to us. However, such actions tell us that we are unable to let go of the past and move on in life, and so we condemn ourselves to repeat the very thing we are trying to disown. I remember the many times in my childhood when our father promised to take us all out for a drive in the country in a friend's car, or to come with us to the swimming baths or to the pictures. Always, it seemed, something came up and he had to break his promise. It felt so depressing to realize that perhaps these were empty promises and so, as a father myself, I always prided myself on keeping my promise and urging my children to keep their word because it was so important to be reliable. However, I felt no satisfaction in keeping my word and reacted out of all proportion when others failed to keep their word to me even though I minimalized my own failures with plenty of plausible excuses! I see that I was trying to make up both for the disappointments I felt as a child and to try and prove that I was a better man than my father. All of this was a game of hurting pride and I needed to repent of my duplicity and try to be me rather than the man I wanted my father to be.

We also need to acknowledge that very often when we have been hurt or deprived in our childhood we work as hard as we can to drown out the memories of those days. It is our way of controlling the feelings inside from exploding, and when we feel threatened we work all the harder and faster. Sadly a lot of our determination to be better, because it is motivated by unhealed wounds, only makes us appear hard and aggressive or too demanding and possessive.

3   Distorted ideas of God

Some years ago I preached a sermon on the power of prayer, but afterwards was challenged by an eighteen-year-old girl who said that she had tried all the forms of prayer I had outlined and none of them had worked. As I tried to defend my sermon, I was quite challenged by her directness, and we came on to the subject of her life with her father. She suddenly became reluctant to talk any further, but with some gentle encouragement she told me something of her story:

My father is an RAF sergeant. He came into my bedroom every week to make a kit inspection of my room. No matter how hard I tried there was always something he found fault with. The one thing I never got right was to clean the windowsill outside of my bedroom window. My father would invariably lift the bottom window and run his index finger along it and then hold up before my eyes this finger smudged with the stain of dirt from outside. He never said a word, he just looked at me as if to say, 'Caught you out again!'

I then asked her, 'And when you pray and say "Our Father who art in heaven", who do you see in your mind's eye?' Quick as a flash she said, 'I see God with three sergeant's stripes on his arm.' 'And who wants to pray to a God like that,' I said, 'who will always greet you with the feeling that he has caught you out again and found fault with you?' Her prayer life was hindered by the fact that she felt that her heavenly Father would act precisely in the same manner as her natural father. This is where the divide between head and heart, between faith and feeling, is often felt the most keenly. Our faith tells us that God is loving, kind and always willing to forgive, but sometimes our feelings tell us that it is not safe to get too close to this father because he might just abuse us or let us down like the last one. Once when I was counselling the wife of a friend she said very strongly that she only really prayed to God and felt nothing for Jesus. As she explored this conviction she began to speak of how it felt to be without close family, especially a brother, because she had been separated from her real brother when she was put in an orphanage as a little girl. In some way her feelings of being alone told her that Jesus mustn't get too close because she might be separated from him too. Better to play safe, and only pray to God who was mighty and distant from her. Her faith was still imprisoned, to some degree, by the little girl's feelings back in that orphanage. It was only after she had received healing for those memories of being deprived of family that she was able to come close to Jesus in a more meaningful way.

It is quite apparent, then, that our feelings can radically

affect our ideas about God. So much so that they can hijack our theological beliefs. This can produce a dysfunctioning of feeling and thought whereby truths believed by faith can produce the exact opposite of what they are designed to convey. For example, for an abuse survivor the idea of being loved and held by the Father may offer anything but security and affirmation. This is often why fellowships which offer a more charismatic style of worship both attract and repel such people. On the one hand they are looking for a security their childhood never offered them, and on the other they are repelled by the offer of intimacy because they cannot separate it from the abuse they received. Therefore we need to bring healing to our feelings rather than try to deny or suppress how we feel or minimize their importance. This work of healing takes the form of uncovering the memory and clarifying its effects upon us and the message it still carries, and then changing its message so that it conforms to the truth we now see and accept by faith. Joseph Sica traces the different ways children experience their parents during the various stages of growing up. He goes on to show how some of these experiences can shape how we look at God:[14]

THE LEGAL GOD	One who keeps an account of what we do. This god waits for us to make a mistake so that he can mark us as losers.
THE GOTCHA GOD	Like a detective in disguise, this god waits for us to step out of line when he pounces upon us and says 'Gotcha!'
SITTING BULL GOD	This god relaxes in a detached yoga-like posture awaiting us to bring homage.
PHILOSOPHER GOD	This is the unmoved mover of the universe, distant and withdrawn. He is much too busy running a vast number of other galaxies to be concerned with our personal lives.
PHAROAH GOD	An unpleasable taskmaster who is always demanding more. Seamands compares him

to the archetypal mafia godfather who says 'measure up or else!'

It does not take too much thought to imagine the terrible human relationships reflected by such projections onto God. With such distortions it is impossible to believe that such a God could love and forgive us or be interested in our personal growth.

Consequently, many Christians live a sort of stunted spirituality because the God they worship is a fraud and an idol. It is not the real God who is the Father who opened heaven and said of his Son for all to hear, 'This is my beloved Son in whom I am well pleased' (Matthew 3:17).

Therefore the route to healing is not to demand orthodoxy of belief and practice, as this will clearly only confirm such distorted images, but to find the original wound and bring the healing Christ into such a place. It involves enabling a person to talk out their feelings and choices in the presence of Jesus. He is able to touch their feelings because he was similarly tested in every way, but without sin (Hebrews 4:15). It is this gift of 'creative space' which throws light upon how the individual chose to respond to such moments, and this is the place where repentance and forgiveness take place as part of the healing change within their lives.

4   Inability to remember

Often one of the signs that we may have need of healing of memories is the fact that we simply cannot remember part of our past. This is quite different from those times that we have forgotten but which we remember upon being prompted. It is not unusual to find certain people who cannot remember a single moment beyond a certain year of their childhood. For some it may be because what lies behind the closed door of memory are things which are too terrible or disturbing to handle. This is where extreme caution needs to be exercised so that we do not prematurely open wounds and find that the emotions within are too strong to handle and so much damage is done. Thankfully, we have the faithful ministry of the Holy Spirit who knows at what pace the individual can work and confront their inner trauma. I have known when working with ritual abuse survivors that the work of healing can take up to five years before the person is able to take full control of their lives again. However, there are times when the unhealed moments in our lives are brought to our attention quite unexpectedly and we are challenged to confront them in the healing power of the Holy Spirit.

Because we sometimes repress such memories this does not mean that we do not live through the trauma of feelings they contain. Invariably we adopt some routine which either disguises the true issues or we display some patterns of behaviour which reflect the emotional scars we carry. Claudia Back says that repression of this kind usually affects the family from which the 'forgotten' experiences have emerged, as well as the new family the individual has created through marriage. This is because the person concerned may still have to go on living with some form of communication with their family. She says that the resultant behaviour usually involves decisions of not to talk, not to trust and not to feel in the presence of such family members.[15] What sometimes develops is a conspiracy to forget on behalf of the family. Every member is pulled into maintaining the status quo and plays their role accordingly. Therefore the unhealed agenda becomes like a communal nightmare, taking the form of unfinished business which will resurface in various ways until it is properly recognized and brought to the place of healing. An example of family conspiracy is found in the story of Joseph and his brothers. The story begins with the growing jealousy and hatred of the brothers towards Joseph, principally for the favouritism shown him by their father Jacob. They also despised him for the arrogance and pride he displayed when he shared insights given to him by God (Genesis 37:3–20). Incidentally, it could be said that the family problem actually began with the favouritism shown by their great-grandfather Abraham towards Ishmael over Isaac. It brought strife and divisions within the Semitic tribes both for Abraham in his day and also down the centuries, as is witnessed by the Palestinian conflict within modern Israel. Isaac never learned from his father's mistake because he showed favouritism towards his athletic son Esau, whereas his wife Rebecca chose to spoil the younger and quieter son Jacob. The consequences of these actions led to twenty years of exile for Jacob and the break up of his family home. Yet neither did Jacob learn from his own bitter experience because he too found a child to show his preference for, and the results of this almost led to family murder. Here we see a classic example of a family conspiracy still in force down to the third generation, if not beyond.

Joseph's brothers had no doubt tried to forget the incident of years before, and doubtless they never talked about their younger brother if they could help it. However, after years of repressed memories, there comes a moment of dawning awareness as they are confronted by this new ruler in Egypt who reminds them of Joseph (Genesis 42:1–24; 43:16–31; 45:1–15). Joseph, unlike his brothers, could not forget. Consequently he gradually begins to bring his brothers to confront their repressed memories. He does this by requiring one of the brothers to be left behind in prison as a guarantee that the youngest, Benjamin, would arrive in Egypt. No doubt the memory of seeing Joseph lowered into a well immediately flashed through their minds, and again the associated feelings of guilt and shame would have resurfaced. All the long-buried secrets they had tried to forget would now engulf them once more.

'For full recovery to take place Joseph needed to hear their acknowledgement of their sin, and they needed to feel his pain.'[16] In order for Joseph to forgive them he needed to know that they owned their responsibility for their actions quite fully and that he too had gained some insight into his own part, and God's, in that long-ago affair (Genesis 45:1–7). It was only when he saw the truth of repentance that Joseph could reveal himself. This is so often the case with our own repressions. It is only when we are enabled to see what actually happened, as opposed to how we feel about what happened, that we can take God's grace and help, come out into the open light of day and live a fuller life. Joseph enabled his brothers to come to terms with the guilty secret which bound them all together. When they too saw it, out came their feelings which had been threatening to boil over for so long (Genesis 45:2–3, 14–15). In many and different ways God brings us to a place in our journey through life where we are given the gift of locating the point of our pain before sharing in the healing he also has to offer.

LOCATING THE POINT OF PAIN

Apart from the above indications that we may be in need of healing of the memories, there are a number of ways by which we are able to locate where our need for inner healing may lie.

A crisis

There are times in our life when some event triggers some other moment or memory and we find ourselves reacting to the former more than the latter. This often explains why we may appear to over-react to a situation. I well remember a friend from some years ago now who had come to the end of his time as a curate in a parish and had just accepted a living to become the minister of a church in another district. Much to his surprise and distress he began to experience feelings of great alarm and fear. He could not find a reasonable explanation for his feelings and they certainly did not appear to be a reaction to his new appointment, to which he looked forward with enthusiasm. However, as he talked about the feelings, they overwhelmed him with great intensity and out of this troubled place he suddenly remembered how, as a baby, his heart had stopped beating more than once and he had to be resuscitated a couple of times before his heartbeat became steady.

'It is almost as if you did not want to be born', I remarked. He instantly replied by saying that he did not feel that it was safe and it made him feel very afraid. We prayed into this whole area of his thinking and feeling, after which he investigated the circumstances surrounding his conception and birth. Some time later he informed me that his mother had told him that she concealed the fact of her pregnancy from her husband for some months because she was afraid he would be troubled by yet another child born to a family already in difficult straits. When the news was broken to him his immediate reaction was to demand an abortion, but he later changed his mind and always loved his youngest child. Strange as it may seem, as a child within his mother's womb, he was aware of his father's response and it had left a scar of fear within his innermost feelings. My friend reported that although his great fears had occurred once or twice before in his life when he was facing other demanding changes, they had immediately subsided as we prayed. To my knowledge he has not experienced those fears ever again down the years. This is not the place to go into detail about primal memories but suffice it to say that there are crises in our lives which tap into the unhealed memories and feelings of other days, and we need to be aware of such things so that we can recognize our need for healing of those memories.[17] The crisis can also take the form of an accident where the shock of impact opens up the force of old memories; or bereavement, where the present loss uncovers aspects of our lives which we may feel we lost due to emotional damage. One person who came to our counselling centre in Leicestershire initially came to talk about the death of a parent. He said that he wanted to cry but somehow he kept getting stuck with a picture of himself as a child going about the home doing lots of work but having no play. He felt that he had in fact been robbed of his childhood. Apparently his parents used him as a pawn in their own marital disputes, and whenever he attempted to share his own ups and downs they had told him to be a man as the family was going through a difficult time. He had left home eventually and become quite successful in his chosen profession. Rarely did he go back to the family home, giving as his excuse the fact that he was so needed at work, and his parents would understand. However, the death of his mother had triggered the feelings of the repressed child and he felt trapped. With work and care he came to the place where he rediscovered his lost childhood feelings; in a way it was the discovery of his little child within which enabled the businessman to cry for his dead mother.

Other crises in life can be unemployment, marriage or ill health, all of which can trigger memories which perhaps share a similar emotional deposit as the present-day event. Should we find ourselves over-reacting to some crisis we encounter, this may be the moment to reflect upon its implications and possibly open the door for the healing of memories.

Dreams

Our dreams so often capture and keep within our unconscious minds those moments and feelings which have been and still are of significance in our lives. The writer of the Song of Songs wrote, 'I sleep but my heart is awake' (Song of Songs 5:2). Of course Hebrew psychology taught that the heart was not just an emotion but the thinking and intuitive mind. It has been demonstrated by researchers such as Nathaniel Kleitman and Bill Dement that generally speaking the dreamer is in control of his or her dreams and is responsible for what they contain. If this is the case then we have to ask why it is we frighten ourselves with nightmares and repetitive dreams which disturb. Most nightmares have the similar feature that just before the worst part of the dream is to occur the dreamer awakes. It is almost as if we are telling ourselves by doing this that we are not yet ready to confront and complete the issue lying within the dream. Therefore all nightmares by definition deal with unfinished business.[18]

I was once approached by an elder of an Evangelical church on Merseyside who had had a dream which was filled with feelings of alarm and fear. In the dream he was looking down at a little boy who was sitting in front of the fire amidst what looked like spilt flour or sugar. He noticed as he reflected on this dream that the furniture in the room was very similar to that in the cottage in which he had once lived when he was four years old. As the young boy was sitting on the floor the door suddenly swung open and into the room came an exceedingly large woman who proceeded to beat him with a steel rod. As the beating continued the dream suddenly ended in a rising crescendo of crying and shouting.

As Frank shared his dream he was aware that he had actually begun to feel what he dreamed and was quite shaken as a result. Slowly he gave himself permission to see that he was in fact the little boy of the dream and that the large woman was of course his mother who had regularly beaten him when he was young. At the time of sharing the dream he was over fifty years old and his mother was approaching eighty years of age. However, he now began to understand how he felt because although he could not think why, he had always been afraid of the little old lady that was now his mother and consequently he was inexplicably reluctant to go home and visit her. He would think of other things which he needed to attend to. Sometimes when he did go home he felt tense and relieved when the time for returning home came. The little boy inside him was still smarting at the beatings. His dream work helped him to locate where the pain stemmed from and in due course he was able to face up to his feelings and find release through the loving power of God in his life. He felt better equipped as a result to go back home with a better spirit and, less than a year after his healing, his mother died.

Therefore we need to respect our dreams but not invest them with more than we should. However, they can often be a way of locating an inner wound that needs to be brought to the Lord for his healing touch.

Counselling

Counselling is an opportunity to work through and clarify how we may be feeling about anything. Once this is done we are in a better place to take appropriate responsibility and action for our growth and healing in God. It is this action which we call ministry. So often when we engage in this kind of process we begin to uncover some deeper awareness of buried and unresolved hurts we may have been carrying. For example a married couple came for a series of counselling sessions with a view to try and save their marriage. Each had their own reasons for being there, part of which was a desire for their partner to see the error of their own ways and to change and subsequently improve their relationship. At one stage in the conversation the husband suddenly interrupted his wife when she was speaking and shouted, 'You treat me just like my mother does; you're always putting me down!' Apparently he had never shared these feelings with his wife before as he was too embarrassed and ashamed. It became the turning-point in their relationship. The husband was really encouraged by the way his wife was prepared to try and understand these feelings and not condemn him for having them. The wife was similarly helped because she had never seen her husband vulnerable and open in this way before. It offered them both a new understanding of each other and although they had many uphill battles to face, they did so together.

Counselling also helps us to understand the different strands of personal material that go into making our individual selves. In doing this we sometimes discover parts of our lives which we have relegated in importance because we feel diminished by having them. It is these silenced voices from our lives which need to be heard in the presence of God and where appropriate challenged, rebuked, forgiven and transformed through the inflowing love of God for us.

Contemplative prayer

I have sometimes found it very helpful in locating which memories need healing to use a form of contemplative prayer. It often helps before sharing in this form of prayer to make sure that the individual is relaxed and at ease. Begin with a prayer inviting the Lord Jesus to oversee the work about to be done and to guide and guard the sharing by his holy presence. In this kind of work we are reflecting almost exclusively upon the client's own material, so we just need to beware that we do not assume that it is infallible at all points. It is, however, the reality which the client is actually living and so may need to be brought to the foot of the cross and examined in the light of God's word and deeds.

Invite the person to see their life rather like a house which has a number of rooms see the figure and Teaching Guide on pages 119–21. We are told in the Bible that Jesus comes to the Church and to each one of us and is like a divine visitor to our house. He knocks on the door and waits to be invited in so that we may have fellowship with him. Focusing on this Scripture we can invite each person to let their faith reach out to Christ Jesus and be aware of him coming to the door of their house and knocking. As you go through this way of praying do allow plenty of time in between each action so that the implications and revelations which God allows can be fully appreciated.

This particular house has three rooms. First, the living room, which represents that part of the house which we allow everyone else to see. It is the public venue of our life in relationship to others. Second, there is an attic which represents that part of our lives influenced by our parents or other authority figures. The final room is the basement, and down there lives our child who carries all the moments of feeling in responding to life.

Taking your time, ask the person to invite Jesus into each room in turn and allow themselves to be aware of particular memories which come to mind as they do this. When the most prominent or powerful memory of thought has come to mind, then literally bring the parent and child figures associated with them in turn, into the living room. Encourage them particularly to note how such figures respond to Jesus in their room and how Jesus, according to their faith, reacts to them. The idea of bringing such memories into the living room is to say that we own these moments as ours and, once we do that, then this is the beginning of healing. Naturally we need to be aware that this may be quite hard work for some people and it might not even be an appropriate method for others because they do not easily work in this fashion. Give plenty of opportunity to see which memories are chosen and encourage them to share them as they happen. Once this form of work is completed then it may be opportune to offer to God in prayer what needs to be released and what needs to be integrated into the individual's life. Whatever insights are gained they should be offered to Christ who is our alpha and omega, the God of all our

LETTING JESUS INTO THE HOUSE OF MEMORIES
(Adapted from original by Ron File)

'Behold I stand at the door and knock!' (Revelations 3:20)

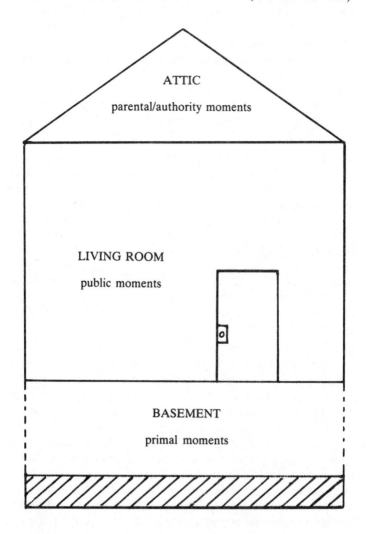

moments, so that he can deliver us from the effects of unhealed wounds and strengthen us to walk in the healing he brings.

MINISTERING INNER HEALING AS WE WALK THROUGH OUR
HOUSE OF MEMORIES

1 *Make a Contract for Work*
Establish confidentiality, pace, staying open.

2 *Invite the Holy Spirit to take Control*
A general offering/opening the door for guided work. NB. Difference between introspection and inner healing is the Holy Spirit at work.

3 *Drawing an Emotional Map*
Cf. Revelations 3:20, the 3 dimensions of the personal house. Helps to focus or choose which particular memory to take up.

4 *Time to Narrate and Feel*
Allow client to speak from their own perspective of the problem. Don't immediately challenge with 'oughts and shoulds'. NB. Often they will speak from the age or stance of the time of the original hurt. This is like finding the child within, loving the child and freeing it so the adult can get on with his or her life.

5 *Recognize the Real Feelings/Memory*
Feelings may need to be given a voice. Don't let sinking feelings become stinking feelings. NB. The cry of dereliction, Own these feelings as yours, it is only then that we can truly choose what to do about them.

6 *Inviting Jesus into Painful Memories*
NB. Be cautious not to be over-directive here. Be supportive, especially in silences.

7 *Confronting the Areas of Bondage*
Take authority over parents' sins.
Break inner voices, vows.

Deliverance from curses.
Proclamation of truth in Jesus.

8 *Filled with the Spirit and Love*
   Asking the Holy Spirit to heal and care where there had
   been hurt and bondage.

9 *The Work of Forgiveness*
   Releasing those to whom you have been bound, etc.
   Release from generational ties, family history patterns.

10 *Thanksgiving and Renewal*
   Establishing new patterns of thinking and behaviour.
   Having Jesus as the focus on all our moments.
   Building on the saving presence of God.

Resting in the spirit

This is not the same thing as what is called being 'slain in the
Spirit', but is rather a surrender of the life to the sovereign
Holy Spirit, trusting him to bring to our awareness the very
scenario in our lives to which he wishes to bring healing. It is
therefore a work of faith and trust, and whatever thoughts
seem to be underlined within us, these are the ones which we
share as a sort of biography of that part of our lives. Whatever
is shared then becomes the focus of prayer for Jesus to be a
healer and a helper. It is not an indulgence in introspection
where we try and uncover and analyse what concerns us. It is
simply sitting or lying comfortably and inviting the Holy Spirit
to present a particular moment in our lives to share in the trust
that he is the guide and that what he shows will be offered for
healing.

Charismatic gifts of knowledge and wisdom

The list of spiritual gifts in 1 Corinthians mentions a number
which are revelatory in nature. These include the word of
knowledge, the word of wisdom (often taking the form of wise
counsel as to how to implement or apply whatever knowledge
God has imparted to a person), prophecy, and discernment of

spirits (1 Corinthians 12:8, 10). When sharing prayer counsel with people it often happens that the Holy Spirit gives some insights as to where ministry should be focused for healing to occur. One such occasion was when I was praying with a woman at a conference about her chronic depression which she had carried ever since she could remember. Suddenly, into my mind came the sentence, 'You have a sister who died when you were young but I want you to know that she lives with me in heaven.' I asked her if she had had a sister who died. Her reaction was immediate; she told me that she had indeed had a sister who was one year older than her but who died when she was about seven years old. That sister had loved her and played with her and given her the attention that she felt she never had from her family. Her death had brought a death blow to her heart she said. Standing at the front of that church I invited her, through Jesus, to give thanks for such a loving sister who would one day be reunited with her. This simple prayer unlocked so much pain and emotion inside her that she had to lie down afterwards as she felt so tired. However, before going home, she came over to tell me that she felt as if a great weight had been lifted off her shoulders. She had literally been carrying death on her heart but the prayer of thanksgiving and the reality of the communion of saints had brought her healing.

One of the exciting things about our generation is the renewal of these gifts within the life and ministry of the Church. Therefore we should be open and expectant for God to share his gifts with us, especially the work of healing the whole person. Let us now finally examine something of the healing process we need to bring to hurting memories which we have uncovered.

HEALING THE MEMORIES THAT HURT

David Benner suggests that there are three main stages in the process of healing a memory: re-experiencing the pain, reinterpreting the hurt and releasing the anger.[19] He suggests that these stages correspond to dealing with the emotional world, the intellectual clarifications and the choices we go on making as a result. It is in this latter department that the work of forgiveness enables us to let out any anger we may still have and then let go of holding on to the pain and the people who gave us such inner wounds. Actually, we must enter this area of healing with the motivation of forgiveness rather than to try and ultimately arrive at the will to forgive. If we are not willing to forgive as we set out, then this journey of discovery often results in frustration and a heightened sense of pain, but nowhere to go for relief. So let us look at how forgiveness threads itself through the process of reliving the past, realizing the whole story and releasing trapped feelings.

1 Reliving the past

We have already mentioned that it is pointless to expect that simply reliving the past will itself bring healing. We must be accompanied by the living Christ who calls us to be forgivers all through the journey of discovery. One of the principal encouragements in this ministry is the fact that Jesus has 'been there before us'. He is the man for all our seasons; in addition to feeling massive pain as he hung upon the cross he also experienced tremendous emotional pain. Nowhere is this more obvious than at the time he grappled with loss and pain in the garden of Gethsemane (Matthew 26:36–46; Luke 22:39–46).

> It was in Gethsemane that Jesus truly came to grips with the cost of forgiveness . . . He wanted to show us how to work through difficult, unfair and usually unasked for assignments in life. The pilgrim walking through a painful family-of-origin recovery process will have to follow the master's path; right through the middle of the pain.[20]

Gethsemane also teaches us that Jesus worked through his feelings and did not avoid them. All the rejection and conflict he had tasted in the past was now being relived as he faced a bigger crisis which had come upon him. Reliving the past is confronting the avoidance of the issue and giving myself permission to taste fully what I may have been denying to myself. This wound must not be healed cheaply.

Reliving the past also affords an opportunity to understand the problem from the perspective of the time and place any hurt was originally felt. Rita Bennett says that if forgiveness is to be effective then it must be offered 'from that time and place'.[21] It is rather like becoming the child that was hurt and offering the forgiveness from the perspective of the child within. Recently I was supervising a counsellor who described the various sessions he had had with his client and that at some point the subject of healing of the memories came up. Apparently, one of the repeated statements that the client had made was her surprise at how much pain she still felt towards her father. 'I thought that I had forgiven him', she kept saying. This was in fact true: as an adult, doing her work of counsel and seeing objectively some of the past, she had gone on to forgive her father. However, it was the little girl inside her who still needed to say to her father, 'I forgive you, Daddy.' After all, it was the little girl of her history that felt and retained all the feelings of rejection that needed healing.

This is also true about the emotions felt in reliving the past. When Frank told his dream of being beaten by his mother (pages 115–6) the feelings he experienced were as if he was that child again. This also becomes abundantly clear when working with peoples' dreams; it does not matter if the dream is very old, they invariably present their feeling material as if it had all just happened a moment ago. This is where the role of a Christian counsellor is so important and so effective; if we allow proper space to listen to another speak from the vulnerability of their times of wounding, then we give respect to their person which helps to undo the stigma and the poison of the wounds they may be carrying.

To re-experience the past also helps to confront our attempts to repress or forget our hurts. Forgiveness is all about letting go, but ironically it also helps us to hold on to those things we need to acknowledge. Only then, when we know their power and place in our past, can we come to God and, through his grace, find the ability to let go forever. We are familiar with the expression 'forgive and forget', but I sometimes think my friend David Smethurst was nearer the truth when he said, 'We need to forgive and remember.'

We must not assume either that the ability to forget is tantamount to having forgiven; it can be a way of avoiding dealing with past hurts. Lewis Smedes said that the test of forgiveness lies with healing the lingering pains of the past and not with forgetting that the past ever happened.[22] Our wounds tie us to the past and if we try and forget them, then we keep the past as a jailor over our present. To relive is a commitment to remember and to forgive.

To relive helps us to deal particularly with people we need to forgive but who are now dead, and we are tempted to think that because of this there can be no healing and no change. The opportunity has gone from us and we feel stuck with an old relation we now feel unable to address. Reliving helps us to speak to such people as if they were still alive because, for us, the memory we are seeking to heal has lived on within our souls.

> I have seen many Christians whose lives were revolutionized when they acknowledged a wrong attitude towards parents, repented of it and made the necessary changes. I remember one man who was convicted of a lifetime of bitterness and hatred towards his father. Although his father was already dead, this man journeyed hundreds of miles to the cemetery where his father was buried. Kneeling beside the grave, he poured out his heart to God in deep contrition and repentance. He did not rise from his knees until he knew his sin was forgiven and he was released from its evil effects.[23]

I call this form of ministry Requiem Healing because it brings together our need to remember those who are now dead and our need to confront the way we still go on relating to them in patterns of behaviour that repeat the painful hold they once exerted over us. So often the nature of this hold over us takes the form of the deceased's lack of involvement within our lives. I have been so blessed when parents have come before the Lord and have acknowledged the right to life of the children that they have lost either through miscarriage or abortion. In many cases the mother carries a deep guilt at this loss of life and the child is buried within the parents' hearts. These times of healing often include moments when such children are named in faith and prayers of repentance for ignoring or not recognizing that such a child is their own and lives within the presence of Jesus who suffers all children to come unto him.[24]

Finally, we need to remind ourselves that we do not go on this journey of reliving unaccompanied; Jesus is our divine Paraclete who walks alongside us. It is his presence with us that gives proper perspective to our faith. For some people, reliving can be very demanding and quite frightening; however, when they are encouraged to focus on the person of Jesus with them in their hurting times, then very often a healing way forward is found. In my book *Healing Dreams* I mentioned the story of Martin who struggled to hide his memories of his father attacking him by blotting out his remembering with repeated bouts of drunkenness. When he was encouraged in his work of reliving, to hold on to his memory, but at the same time to 'fix his eyes on Jesus, the author and perfecter of his faith' (Hebrews 12:2), his tremendous fear of his father began to change. He saw Jesus holding out forgiveness to his father, and with some trepidation he thought he would do the same. So he said, 'Father, I forgive you, because you did not know what you were doing.' This was very appropriate because Martin's father had been mentally disturbed and in such a state had violently attacked all his family.

Whilst this form of ministry does involve some degree of visualization, it is not the main focus of the ministry. What is important is that the individual relates the Jesus he or she knows by faith to those inner moments of which Jesus has not yet been made Lord. It is perfectly orthodox and possible to do this because Jesus holds all our times in his hands; he is the alpha and omega, the first and last of every moment in time and eternity (Psalm 31:15; Revelation 1:8, 21:6, 22:13). Thus we can present to the Lord those shadowy places we carry within our hearts and by faith see how his divine presence changes the old story and begins to make all things new. It is not an over-simplification to ask a person to retell their hurting memory from the perspective of Jesus being present within it, because, in a very real sense, he was there, unseen at the time but nonetheless ready to heal and save if only we had eyes to see him. As the faith story is told so faith is released and the power to be healed is made ours through the grace of God's loving presence.

Therefore, reliving the past is not wallowing in our hurt feelings but confronting the roots of our hurts and where possible offering forgiveness so that we can go free into a freer future. We may not lose our painful or uncomfortable feelings overnight, but they will no longer exercise the same kind of tyrannizing power over us.

2   Realizing the whole story

If we do not come to terms with our unhealed memories then we are in danger of continually distorting the past because we only look backwards through the focus of our feelings. In healing of the memories we are given an opportunity to appreciate all the aspects of the story. I used to complain constantly that my father never loved me or acted like a father to me. I was hurt and bitter but as I shared it with a counsellor I began to appreciate Dad's needs as well as my own. I saw that his father was a remote and distant figure, as was his grandfather before him. I could not be so bitter when I saw that my father was as much a victim of circumstance as I was. Incidentally, I received even more healing into this part of my life quite recently when my Mum suddenly passed away. Along with my brothers and sisters we cried and poured out our grief at this great loss that we all felt because Mum had been the most formative influence for good upon our childhood. Very simply, I realized in my crying that I was loved very much by my mother and that my longing for my Dad to be a father had obscured this truth. I was suddenly set free from the chronic need for my father as I felt all those many memories of Mum's love come flowing back into my heart. It felt a rich blessing to me in my sadness and although I do love my father and would like him very much to love me, I no longer have this deep unhealing cry to be loved by him. This was a very releasing insight for me personally. Also my focus began to shift from my own feelings to include my actions as well, some of which I needed to repent of and receive forgiveness from God. Sometimes we remain unhealed because we nurture the picture of ourselves as victim and the other as monster; we are disturbed when we see that we too may need to be forgiven for nursing our bitterness and in some cases building a whole life-style around it.

I remember my next-door neighbour, Jenny, coming to a Christian celebration with me one evening. As we drove home she calmly told me that at long last she had learned to forgive herself and that this now made it possible to marry a new man who had come into her life and that of her little five-year-old boy. She went on to explain what she meant. Her first marriage was a disaster because her husband would beat her violently; it was only when he started on their son that she decided enough was enough and she left him and later obtained a divorce. However, she told everyone how bad her husband had been but she totally ignored how she had goaded him on sometimes and rather enjoyed the way she could manipulate him in a rather sick way. She had felt trapped with her conflicting feelings and this immobilized her from making any new commitments in her life. However, in the service that night the preacher had mentioned that sometimes we are unable to forgive others because we refuse to forgive ourselves. This too needed to be repented of.

Another important aspect of identifying the whole story is to begin to see the problem which wounded us reduced to a more manageable size. One person who was working through a whole childhood of abuse suddenly realized that the man who had done all those things was just a little old man and not a huge ogre. That person shouted out, 'You can't do that to me ever again. I won't let you.' He had been responding to his childhood only as a child, but through the work he did he separated the past from his present and saw that he need not be afraid any more. Once he had come to terms with his new liberty he was then able truly to forgive his uncle and hold no more hatred towards him. In one sense, this is what Jesus did from the cross; he forgave because he could see the whole story and he knew that they did not really know what they were doing.

Because we understand more of the story we can also, with the help of God, confront and refute the punch line such moments have delivered to us. One woman who had felt ashamed and unclean all her life because she had been raped by a gang of youths suddenly realized in a time of prayer that she was innocent. She had had years of reliving the awful day in nightmares which re-ran the whole episode. However, when we prayed together she was made aware by God of the helplessness of Jesus upon the cross and of how he too had been physically abused. She almost sang out the words, 'I'm not dirty! I'm not dirty!' She then spoke to her attackers as if they were in the room with us (they had actually been given room in her heart), and said to them, 'You are wrong about me. You had no right to do what you did to me. I'm not guilty and God says so.' Such a moment of revelation and challenge enabled her to pick up the pieces of her life and begin to trust people, especially men. She let go of punishing herself and let go of those boys – they were not really men – and went free. It is when we can forgive, once in possession of more of our story, that we in effect say to the past, 'I will no longer give you the power to wound me.'[25] This does not mean that the sins of those who have done us evil are forgiven by God, but it does mean that when we forgive, the power of sin to continue to wound and shape our lives is broken. What is more, it can also present us with the opportunity to speak words of blessing to others whereas before we could only speak ill of them. Was it not Jesus who blessed others when they cursed him? This too is part of the cross of growing up into full maturity in Jesus Christ.

3   Releasing trapped feelings

Healing of the memories inevitably brings us into contact with very strong emotions and they need to be properly handled.

Perhaps two equal and opposite ways of wrongly handling emotions is either just to vent them in any fashion or to deny them any expression at all. Benner is critical of the general role of a therapist who encourages his or her clients just to get in touch with their anger. He is not against working with such strong feelings but he is concerned that we do not think that venting feelings is the object of the exercise; such is only a means to an end, it is not the end itself.[26] It is precisely here that some people can feel stuck with their feelings because they have vented them but have not moved any further on in their lives. Forgiveness is the antidote to this problem.

It is important to realize that we do have a right to our feelings because they describe where we are living within. To deny such feelings is to lie to ourselves and live in an unreality. Of course this also means that we cannot forgive or be forgiven because we are in effect saying, there is nothing to forgive. If we go on repressing such strong feelings then we will become ill not only mentally but also physically. We need to take the middle road then and work with our anger. This is not so easy for Christians because we understand from the scriptures that we are to put away all anger and bitterness if we would live godly in Christ (Ephesians 4:31). This usually means that we try and bury our anger inside. However, the matter is further complicated by the fact that Jesus got angry and was not averse to showing it to others. Consider how he stood at the entrance to the temple, watching what was going on there and all the time making a whip with which he wrecked the tables of the money-lenders as he literally threw them out of God's house (John 2:13–16). This is a world away from the gentle Jesus meek and mild imagery that we were often fed at Sunday School and in many a sermon. There is also the Pauline injunction to be angry and sin not nor to let the sun go down on our anger (Ephesians 4:26). What this means of course is that we are not to let our anger fester within our lives but to find some way of dealing with it properly. Matthew and Dennis Linn write that anger is rather like a motor which should drive us to love Christ, whose anger was used to confront sin and injustice.[27] For so many with wounded pasts the road to freedom is paved with freeing the feelings of outrage and anger towards those who brought the wound. It is regaining a sense of the injustice of what had been done to them and is therefore a bid for their right to live a whole life as opposed to a damaged one.

> I was angry with my friend:
> I told my wrath; my wrath did end.
> I was angry with my foe.
> I told it not; my wrath did grow.[28]

There are a number of ways in which we can share our hurt feelings. We can tell them to a counsellor or we can write them in a letter to those who have hurt us (but of course the letter is not actually sent but read out as a way of making sure the feelings are properly voiced and heard). They can become the subject of our prayers to God. We can find our equivalent of a Gethsemane, a place where we can pour out our feelings. I once advised a friend who felt his feelings of anger were boiling over to go into the middle of the local park and let it out in a great shout. Then he was to come and share with me how he was then going to deal with his feelings in a fuller and more healing way. For the sharing of feelings like this it is necessary, once they have been owned and voiced, that they are then offered to God for healing through forgiveness. It is only after such feelings have been fully owned that they can be properly released. Yet we must also realize that forgiveness does not mean that we ignore or excuse what has happened, that is to pretend as well as to diminish our own pain. Yet forgiveness does mean that we are no longer being dominated by our past; we are free to choose life and life more abundantly in Christ.

7

Deliverance and Forgiveness

If you forgive anyone, I also forgive him. I have forgiven in the sight of Christ for your sake, in order that Satan might not outwit us. For we are not unaware of his schemes.
2 Corinthians 2:10–11

One of the key elements in setting people free from old agenda in their lives is the power of forgiveness. This is no less true for the whole arena of spiritual warfare into and out of which Jesus offers us his many victories. In writing to the Corinthian church, Paul is anxious that a certain matter of discipline does not degenerate into a slough of despond whereby Satan would gain a grip not only on the life of an individual but in the church itself. We are not sure about the actual matter under review by Paul but it is more than likely concerning the person mentioned in his first letter (1 Corinthians 5:1–13) who had committed incest with his mother. Apparently this person had been removed from the fellowship of the church as a form of discipline. However, he had repented and sought forgiveness but, not having received it, was on the point of despair. So Paul wishes now to bring full healing and restoration of this man to the church. He points out that the sins he had committed were not so much a personal offence to him but were a cause of grief to the whole church (2 Corinthians 2:5ff). But now is the time for love and forgiveness, and so the apostle directs that the person be informed of his forgiveness and his restored place within the fellowship. Failure to do this would offer Satan some kind of hold over them all.

This whole passage, therefore, offers us an insight into forgiveness being both a gift of grace as well as a weapon of warfare. Paul repeats this aspect of forgiveness and battle when he speaks of the 'weapons of righteousness' (2 Corinthians 6:7). It is our right standing before God through Jesus Christ that gives us confidence to exercise the authority and power of Jesus. The man who committed incest would be all too familiar with the accusation of having sinned and being beyond further hope. His forgiveness and restored righteousness would enable him to know that he had sinned but that his sins had been lifted away and that he now stood once more in fellowship with God and his church. It is those who know that they have been forgiven and cleansed who can confidently witness and testify, to the devil himself if necessary, that evil has no claim or power over their lives anymore. It was by the blood of the Lamb and their word of testimony that the faithful overcame the great dragon in the battle for heavenly superiority (Revelation 12:11). Consequently we can see how forgiveness is a strategic weapon and healing step for those times when we need to be delivered from the grasp of the evil one.

Coming back to Paul's letter to the Corinthians we can now see how important it was that the church learned to forgive and reinstate the man they had formerly disciplined. Warren Wiersbe writes that where there is an unforgiving spirit in a congregation because sin has not been dealt with in a biblical manner, it gives Satan a 'beachhead' from which he can operate within the church.[1] As a result Paul is concerned to teach the church about the nature of spiritual warfare and the place of forgiveness in successfully combating it. There is not room in this book to give a full examination to this subject of combat. We shall therefore offer a brief survey of the battle in which the Christian is engaged and how forgiveness is an integral part of our conquest of evil through our Lord Jesus Christ.[2]

The three traditional enemies that Christians combat are the world, the flesh and the devil (and his armies). This is a useful reminder; when we are speaking of the need for deliverance we are referring not just to demonic powers but also to deliverance from the hold of sinful flesh and the spirit of the world in which we live. The word for deliverance, *rhyomai*, means 'to rescue from' or 'to preserve'. This is the word used in Matthew's version of the prayer which Jesus taught his disciples to use regularly, 'Deliver us from the evil one' (Matthew 6:13). It comes as part of the passage on spiritual warfare and forms a conclusion to the ministry of forgiveness: 'Forgive us our debts as we also have forgiven our debtors, and lead us not into temptation but deliver us from the evil one.' John Richards says that the term teaches us that it is better to think of deliverance as being 'to God', rather than 'from the Devil'.[3] As such it underlines that deliverance is not an end in itself if it is to be effective and lasting; it is part of the whole work of Christ and therefore cannot and must not be exercised apart from repentance towards God and faith in Jesus Christ.

THE WORLD

The most significant Greek word for 'world' is *kosmos* and it basically means 'order' or 'arrangement'. As a theological term it portrays human society as a system warped by sin and under the control of demonic powers. Satan himself is called 'the God of this age' (2 Corinthians 4:4) who entices people to follow the ways of the world as he is the ruler of the kingdom of the air (Ephesians 2:2). Fred Dickason says that the term 'world' refers to the spirit of the age that rejects the true God and sets up a counterfeit life and substitute religion with the creature at the centre.[4] This is certainly borne out by the many references in the New Testament, which portrays the world being at variance and in open rebellion to the rule of Christ. For example, the wisdom of the world does not understand God's wisdom; it is regarded as unspiritual and of the devil (1 Corinthians 2:6ff; James 3:15). It was the rulers of the world who crucified the Lord of glory and so declared their opposition to the will of God (1 Corinthians 2:8). Christians are not to be conformed to the world (Romans 12:2); to be the world's friend is to live in enmity with God (James 4:4). Yet Jesus has come to take away the sin of the world (John 3:16–17) even though it will hate him and his followers (John 15:18–19; 17:14; 1 John

3:13). Consequently the Christian Church is called to battle against the spirit at work in the world, and, like Christ, become the light that those who live in such darkness need to see and follow. The world is under the control of the evil one (1 John 5:19) and as such it 'portrays human society as a system warped by sin, tormented by beliefs and desires and emotions that surge blindly and uncontrollably'.[5] However, with the coming of Christ, Satan's rule is broken and the kingdom of God is now established.

Entrance to this kingdom is described as a work of deliverance.

> Joyfully give thanks to the Father who has qualified you to share in the inheritance of the saints in the kingdom of light. For he has rescued ['delivered'] us from the kingdom of darkness and brought us into the kingdom of the Son he loves, in whom we have redemption, the forgiveness of sins. (Colossians 1:12–14)

This is an obvious reference to salvation and it is also a work of deliverance from the influence of Satan's rule upon the unredeemed. This does not necessarily mean that every non-Christian is demonized but it does mean that there is a need of deliverance from a darkened and distorted life. Sometimes the level of influence does extend to the presence of one or more evil spirits at work within that person's life, and therefore the work of deliverance will include casting out such powers in the power of Jesus. The important thing to notice is that deliverance from the world is coupled with redemption and forgiveness of sins.

At the heart of this work of deliverance is a radical change of direction from that of the spirit of the age, which is demonic, to that of Christian discipleship. It is precisely here that we are given the gift of repentance. Thomas Brooks emphasizes that this is not principally a human initiative but an exercise of God's power in breaking all other powers at work in us.[6] The result is that the sinner's whole life is set on the road of transformation. 'First his heart and then his life; first his person, then his practice and conversation.'[7] Such repentance and forgiveness may also include acts of penance whereby the good intention to live a new life is demonstrated in the desire to heal and restore the damage inflicted upon others by sinful living. It may take the form of confessing to particular areas of difficulty and seeking ministry and help to overcome them and find healing. Or it may consist of spiritual exercises to deepen a person's devotion to being a disciple of Jesus. Peter Lombard described penance as the occasion of a new freeing, as in the unbinding of the already risen Lazarus.[8] Here he is focusing on the fact that, although already delivered to new life, the Christian goes deeper into that new life when he confesses his sins and need of God. This also cuts through the chords that have bound him to the old life and dominion of Satan. Leon Suenens takes up this theme and says that the sacrament of penance or reconciliation is more than a sacrament of forgiveness; not only does it efface sin, but it gives grace and a power of resistance in the struggles yet to come. It frees us from sin which gives the forces of evil their ascendency over us.[9]

Neither must we confine this whole issue of deliverance from the world merely to a private journey through life. Such personal forgiveness and healing also awakens us to the need to confront the structural sins and influences of evil within the world. This is surely what is happening when the eighth-century prophets of Israel linked the failure to do justice to the poor within the land with political and military defeats (Hosea 7:1; Amos 5:11–17). The Church too has a calling to proclaim the good news to the poor, and this surely entails confronting the issues of justice and peace within our societies. Naturally this is not always welcomed by the powers that be, both natural and supernatural. Notice the reaction by some Government ministers to the Church of England's *Faith in the City* report which pointed out the appalling conditions of the modern city-dweller in the United Kingdom. They accuse the Church of meddling in affairs which do not concern them. We take on the whole nexus of structural sin and its powers when we confront the social and environmental evils of our world. And like the Old Testament prophets, we may have to confess publicly the sins of our society as our own if we would have

the mercy and forgiveness of God and see the revivals which
we long for.

THE FLESH

In the Old Testament the flesh is presented as being not particularly evil but rather a reflection of frail humanity which shall
some day pass away: 'He remembered that they were but flesh,
a passing breeze that does not return' (Psalm 78:39; cf. Jeremiah 17:5, 7). The term in the New Testament has the same
usage as that in the Old Testament, but in the Pauline Epistles
a more sinister aspect is developed. According to Paul, human
nature is not only frail and weak, it is also twisted and tangled:
'Human perspectives, human understanding, and human efforts
are actually hostile to the perspective, understanding, and plan
of God. We are morally inadequate, and we are driven toward
rebellion.'[10] There are a number of striking pictures which Paul
gives to illustrate how the flesh is opposed to the rule of God.

In Romans 7 he describes in detail that the struggle to walk
in holiness is constantly being jeopardized by a rebelliousness
within his own humanity. He concludes that there is nothing
good in his flesh or sinful nature, as the NIV translates the
term *sarx* (Romans 7:18). This opposition to holiness is further
described in Galatians 5 where Paul lists the bad fruit of the
flesh as being sexual immorality, impurity and debauchery,
idolatry and witchcraft; hatred, discord, jealousy, fits of rage,
selfish ambition, dissensions, factions and envy; drunkenness,
orgies, and the like (Galatians 5:19–21). He points out that the
flesh is constantly at war with the spirit and that the way of
victory for the Christian is to crucify the works of the flesh
within us (Galatians 5:17–18, 24). The way of crucifixion is to
live in the Spirit; to be controlled by the life and power of the
Holy Spirit within us (Galatians 5:25; Romans 8:3–11).

One of the ways in which this walk is maintained is the
continuous practice of the ministry of forgiveness. This is what
Paul was saying when he wrote, 'Do not grieve the Holy Spirit
of God with whom you were sealed for the day of

redemption . . . Be kind and compassionate to one another,
forgiving each other, just as in Christ God forgave you' (Ephesians 4:30–2). If I am to forgive another's sins against me it
means that I also recognize my need and reception of God's
forgiveness of my sins. Not to forgive is to slip back into the
old ways of the flesh. In this same Ephesian passage about
being careful not to return to the ways of the flesh, the apostle
describes how the flesh can become a foothold for the Devil to
gain an influence in our lives. Again let me point out that
this does not automatically mean that a demonic presence has
entered a person's life, but if the condition is left to worsen
then it can become a real possibility.

> He gives place – literally claim or practical ground – to
> Satan's activity in his life. Giving way wilfully to practise sins
> of the flesh gives occasion for Satan to have his way in a
> believer's life. Although all legal claim of Satan against us
> was cancelled at the cross, a believer's wilfull indulgence in
> fleshly sins gives the enemy a place or claim against us which
> he will be quick to exploit.[11]

The practice and quest for forgiveness is our way of recognizing that something is wrong and that we need renewal in
the Holy Spirit. Forgiveness is also a celebration of the power
of grace over the darkness of evil, because evil will hold and
bind whereas forgiveness releases. Again this is often why it is
good to have someone who in the name of Christ can hear our
confession and remind us of the forgiveness of God to us. Often
when I am praying with people who confess I like to tell them,
face to face, that their sins are forgiven. Most of the books
which outline a method of deliverance and healing are very
careful to include in the liturgy of freedom an opportunity for
the individual to give God praise that he has forgiven them
and set them free from the works of the flesh (see the forgiveness exercise in Appendix 1). More and more Evangelicals and
Charismatics are using some of the healing rites more familiar
to the Orthodox or Roman Catholic Churches because they
powerfully help to convey the activity of God's deliverance and
forgiveness. Leanne Payne, for example, in her work of inner

healing, encourages those who are seeking forgiveness and healing from years of abuse to be sprinkled with holy water as an act of faith to underline that they are made clean through the blood of the Lamb. This is often accompanied by manifestations of demonic presence which react to the symbolic use of the water and a subsequent deliverance follows. The use of the signing with the sign of the cross, as at believer's baptism in the Anglican and Roman Catholic Churches, often helps to focus upon the power of Calvary to bring deliverance and forgiveness. Also the anointing with oil can provide a gentle but quiet opportunity for the Holy Spirit to come and refresh and renew that believer with a new outpouring of the Spirit. These are not magical acts which contain the power to help in and of themselves but are vehicles for the Holy Spirit to link the grace of God with our faith in bringing the blessings of God.

Our battle with the flesh is a continuous one for as long as we live and therefore the ministry of forgiveness is to effect continuous deliverance from the influences of darkness within this world. However, it is not a depressing ministry as it constantly reminds us of our need of God and the supply of his grace and Holy Spirit to work within us so that each day we grow into his marvellous likeness and that one day we shall be like him because we shall see Christ face to face.

THE DEVIL

Put on the full armour of God so that you can take your stand against the devil's schemes. For our struggle is not against flesh and blood, but against the rulers, against the authorities, against the powers of this dark world and against the spiritual forces of evil in the heavenly realm.

Ephesians 6:11–12

Paul leaves us in no doubt about who is the real enemy that Christians are fighting when seeking to present the good news

as well as grow into all that God has for them; it is the Devil
and his dark forces of evil. He wishes to remind and focus the
attention of the Ephesian church upon the fact that whatever
difficulties they face, humanly speaking, behind the scenes and
manipulating such opposition to the church is a world of evil
spiritual powers of various degrees and functions. Of course
this is not the first time that the Devil has been mentioned in
this letter (Ephesians 2:2; 4:27). Paul is giving the complete
picture of spiritual warfare as being at one level against those
whose lives are darkened by evil and, at a deeper and sometimes hidden level, against the spiritual powers of darkness.
This is not always so readily accepted by some Christians today
who suggest, for example, that principalities and powers could
be a reference to the secular powers which have been corrupted
and become a source of moral decay. For a useful summary of
these arguments and a clear presentation that these powers are
indeed supernatural and evil, you might like to read the relevant section in John Stott's book *God's New Society*.[12] It is
important, however, that we take spiritual warfare very
seriously, especially if we seek to free and heal those who have
become ensnared by such forces. The late Dr Martin Lloyd
Jones said that one of the main causes of the ill state of the
Church today is the fact that the Devil is being forgotten. 'All
is attributed to us; we have become so psychological in our
attitude and thinking. We are ignorant of this objective fact,
the being, the existence of the Devil, the adversary, the accuser
and his fiery darts.'[13] We must balance up this statement by
saying that we also need to learn to discern the difference
between the need for deliverance from evil and a need for
counselling or even psychiatric care. This is not always apparent
as the symptoms can appear to be very similar. Nevertheless,
we can train ourselves to be aware of those distinguishing
features which are an indication that we are dealing with a
demonic power.[14]

There have been a number of ways in which the demonic
influence upon people has been presented. The most general
is to speak in terms of a threefold progression of spiritual
warfare, such as temptation, oppression and finally possession.

Michael Harper, in his book on *Spiritual Warfare*, speaks of three forms of attack, such as a frontal assault, a siege or blockade and finally an invasion or occupation.[15] I think these are very helpful ways to identify both how the individual perceives his or her struggle with the enemy, as well as suggest the different levels of demonic influence there may be. It is true that the scriptures themselves do not quite make this distinction and treat all manifestations of demonic presence with the same response of casting out the evil spirit(s). However, there are some clues as to the difference in level of encountering demonic power; Paul himself uses two significant words when he speaks of 'foothold' (Ephesians 4:27) and 'strongholds' (2 Corinthians 10:4). This does suggest some difference in the size of the problem or the possible strength of the demons being confronted. Matters are not helped when the term *daimonizomenos* is always translated as 'demon possessed', as this suggests that every case may be of the 'legion' dimension, when this is plainly not so in the Gospels. This is not to deny the strength of demonic influence in the lives of others such as the young lad of Mark 9 who at first glance appeared to have epilepsy. Yet it is quite obvious that the majority of those described as having deliverance in the Gospels do not carry the same weight of demonic influence as that sad man restored by Jesus to his right mind (Luke 8:26–35). The term is better translated as 'having a spirit' or 'bothered by a spirit'. This helps us to appreciate that whereas deliverance is the standard response to setting free those under demonic influence, the size of the battle and the level of the problem can vary. It also helps us to understand that under this approach to the situation we can see that Christians may well need deliverance ministry also. I do not think that a true born-again believer will be in the same position as the man called Legion. This would imply the total ineffectuality of the Holy Spirit, but I do believe that through unrepented sin or repeated sinning we give a foothold to our deadly enemy. We should not be surprised by this; after all, we have already noted that conversion itself is described as a work of deliverance from the kingdomship of darkness. Jesus even forewarned Peter that he would come under demonic influence when he would deny Jesus. The clear implication is that Satan would be able to get a hold of his life in some way but that Peter would come to repentance and be set free (Luke 22:31). So it seems that the doorway to all forms of demonic influence in our lives is the fundamental issue of our sinfulness and our unwillingness or inability to confront our sins and their effects and find the way to freedom and healing. As Leon Suenens said:

> What makes us (that is Christians) slaves of the powers of evil is not normally demonic possession . . . It is sin and its hold on us which makes us slaves and allows perverse influences to become more and more harmful. So deliverance is basically and primarily deliverance from the sin in us.[16]

There is not enough space in this book to examine in more detail the nature of spiritual warfare or the various ways in which demonic powers gain a hold over peoples' lives. I have dealt with this subject elsewhere,[17] but it is interesting to note that all who have written on the subject of deliverance include the need for repentance and forgiveness as a necessary first step to freedom. John writes in his first Epistle, 'If we confess our sins, he is faithful and just and will forgive us our sins and purify us from all unrighteousness' (1 John 1:7). Here the subject of forgiveness is linked to cleansing. Often I have prayed with people who have been involved with the occult and who have consequently registered some difficulties in their Christian growth. One of the ways we have worked together is that I have invited them specifically to confess and renounce the occult involvement they, or even their parents before them, have had. Once this is done, on the authority of the word of God, I assure them that they are indeed forgiven and that we can be open to the Holy Spirit to cleanse them of the unrighteous effects of their former sins. In fact I make this a matter of prayer and specifically command that the power and presence of any hold of unrighteousness be broken and removed from their lives. It is here that sometimes the struggle with a demonic spirit is manifested, whereupon I repeat the prayer of deliverance unless there are other sinful issues which also need to be confessed and dealt with first. Naturally, any prayer of deliverance must be followed up with the necessary ministry of discipline or counsel to ensure that this kind of foothold or stronghold is not repeated. This is surely what is meant when Jesus says that it is not enough to sweep a person's life clean of evil without filling up that void with the Spirit and purposes of God. If this is not done then that demon seems to have a right to return and bring further bondage, and is often accompanied by other spirits to make the last state even worse than the first (Matthew 12:43–5).

Forgiveness therefore entitles us to receive the righteousness of Christ to release us from our enemy's hold and to ensure that we have a shield through which Satan cannot penetrate. Forgiveness actually connects us up with the battle of the cross, because the shed blood of Christ to cleanse us from all sin and the disarming of the spiritual powers over mankind both meet there (cf. Romans 5:9–11; Colossians 2:15). Consequently, Satan cannot stand upon redemption ground because it is precisely there that his power was broken. William Gurnall, in his classic work on warfare, echoes this when he points out that the breastplate of righteousness mentioned in Paul's list of Christian armoury is indeed a weapon of our holiness which gives us the power to be more than a conqueror. 'Your holiness is what the devil wants to steal from you . . . he will allow a man to have everything, or be anything, rather than be truly and powerfully holy.'[18]

Another model to understand the connections between forgiveness and deliverance is that of 'binding and loosing'. The term for binding, *deo*, carries the general meaning of imprisonment or limitation. Amongst other things it is used in relationship to spiritual warfare.[19] When he spoke of destroying Satan's kingdom, Jesus mentioned that the preparation for successful deliverance from the power of the enemy is to first bind the strong man or demonic spirit with which a person may be currently battling (Matthew 12:25–9; cf. Revelation 20:2 and binding Satan in the abyss). It is quite possible, therefore, that when seeking to heal and free people from the effects of certain life experiences or of sinful life-styles, we encounter the hold of demonic spirits which block the entrance into full healing and release. These forms of bondage must therefore be recognized and broken if healing is to occur. This certainly seems to be the case of the woman who battled with eighteen years of sickness, which Jesus described as being the result of the Devil's binding hold upon her (Luke 13:10–16). The form of ministry which Jesus exercised to heal her is not the usual form of prayer or command to be healed, but the command that she be 'loosed'.

Before proceeding in this direction, however, we must engage the person in some counselling so that there is proper space given to determining if there is a demonic spirit or hold at work which needs breaking in the power of the Holy Spirit. If in the course of counselling a person for healing I discover that he or she has been involved in the occult, then I suggest that they go through a form of repentance and renunciation as the first steps to binding any demonic influence in their lives, before loosing them from any effects of such a hold. As the loosing element may well take the form of confronting and battling with spiritual powers over the right of access to a person's life, it is vital that they be assured of, and indeed say that they receive, the forgiveness which Jesus gives to all those who truly repent.

At other times, when working with the victims of physical or ritual abuse, the pain and the distorted life-style for living with that pain is often controlled by a demonic spirit. Alongside this form of bondage is the victim's conviction that it is their fault they are in such a mess because they must have done something in their childhood to deserve it, or they tell themselves they did not do enough to try and escape the situation. The way to freedom so often takes the form where the demonic hold or activity is bound in the name of Jesus and silenced and commanded no longer to harm that person. It is in this interim period that much of the work of forgiveness now takes place. The work of the Devil has been recognized and the individual has a measure of freedom in which to acknowledge their desire to be set free and healed. It is here that the whole subject of needing to forgive themselves for getting involved and staying involved with evil can be dealt with. There may be an opportunity to begin to forgive the perpetrators who dealt them so much pain and distortion. Forgiving them helps to dismantle any hold such people may have over their memories. We begin to see them less as monsters and more as people who need also to be set free from the power of darkness in their lives. It also means that we begin to understand them in proper proportion and they cease to be such a great terror to us. Not to forgive means that whatever wound or hurt being handled in ministry still lays open to manipulation by the enemy, precisely because we have chosen to retain both the past event and our decision to hold it against another. So we must not rush over the subject of forgiveness as if it is a minor hurdle in healing, but give it proper consideration and preparation. A helpful resource for this occasion is to use the baptismal liturgy of the church. The following is an adapted form of this familiar rite:

Do you renounce the devil and all his works in your life?
I do.

Do you renounce all your sinful desires which have drawn you away from the love of Jesus Christ?
I do.

Do you renounce . . . (here mention either any occultic involvement or any person's or demonic spirit's hold in your life)?
I do.

It is important of course that after saying this there follow prayers of repentance and forgiveness, before going on to loose or remove such internal holds of bondage from a person's life. Leanne Payne, incidentally, reminds us that in focusing upon the need for forgiveness as an essential ingredient for proper healing and deliverance, we do not make the mistake of forgiving evil (*per se*), or Satan or the demonic spirits we may be battling against.[20] A basic approach to deliverance including forgiveness, binding and loosing could be the following:

1 Counselling which would examine and consider the prob-

lems the client is experiencing. This would help to identify some of the barriers to healing and growth in God and clarify where the work of the enemy foothold or stronghold is located.

2 Binding of the powers of evil from exercising further influence within that person's life. When Jesus did this he silenced the evil spirits and commanded them not to harm that person any more.

3 Time to repent of and confess personal involvement and response to whatever issues are involved. There may also be a need to forgive oneself for holding any hurts against others or for getting involved in some forbidden activities. It is important during this time that the fact of Christ's forgiveness and cleansing is pronounced on the authority of the word of God and in faith in God's grace. The client is encouraged to pray extemporary prayers of thanks and praise for such forgiveness. You may like to use the form of forgiveness exercise found in Appendix 1.

4 The prayer of deliverance where the hold of the demonic spirit is loosed in the power and authority of Jesus Christ. Before beginning this prayer it is advisable to encourage the client to renounce such spirits and forbid them any rights to their lives ever again. It may be helpful to use another person in this time of prayer providing that the client is happy about this. It is also wise to inform the minister and invite him or her to be present if he or she is not already. This prayer is also to include forbidding the evil spirit to return (cf. Jesus' actions with the young boy in Mark 9:25).

5 Invite the Holy Spirit to fill all those areas now exposed and released through forgiveness and deliverance. This is to extend the reign of the kingship of Christ into those parts which were formerly under the powers of darkness.

6 Have further counselling and healing for those memories and hurts now they have been freed from the added complication of spiritual warfare. Now that the client is more aware of the way that the enemy gained access to their past agenda they are more able to protect themselves from being so easily vulnerable to domination. This may take the form of inner healing work or some exercise in replacing the distorted impressions of life with readings from Scripture which outline the love of God and the life of holiness and freedom he offers to his disciples. Out of this may come fresh material for forgiveness.

7 Encouragement to walk in newness of life which will include the discipline of participation in worship, fellowship and the sacrament of Holy Communion.

We can see, therefore, that forgiveness is a powerful ministry of release from bondage, as well as a weapon in the armoury of righteousness which provides Christians with strong ground to confront the powers of darkness and break their hold over them.

8

Healing the Land Through Forgiveness

*The whole creation is eagerly waiting for God to reveal his
sons . . . it still retains the hope of being freed, like us,
from its slavery to decadence, to enjoy the same freedom
and glory as the children of God. From the beginning till
now the entire creation, as we know, has been groaning in
one great act of giving birth.*

Romans 8:19–22 (Jerusalem Bible)

This final chapter is more of an opportunity to explore and
reflect upon our Christian ministry to the very earth and land
upon which we live. There is now a wave of interest in the
whole subject of the earth as a living organism and our need
to both conserve 'her' natural resources and wild life, as well
as recognize the earth's ministry to create the best environment
possible to sustain all forms of life. The name popularly given
by the originators of this theory is 'the Gaia Hypothesis'.[1] Gaia
was a Greek earth goddess and the reintroduction of this term
just over twenty years ago has served to bring together an
amorphous group, all concerned about protecting our environment; they range from scientific theorists to New Agers who
have connected up a range of pagan and pseudo-Christian spiri-
tualities with conservation concerns. It is this volatile mixture of
science and religion which has confused the Christian Church.
Loren Wilkinson and others plead that the Church does not
engage in a wholesale rejection and refusal to participate in
discussions of environmental issues as was done by the Evangelical Church in Brazil in response to the earth summit held
in Rio de Janiero in 1992.[2] The truth of the matter is that the

Bible does in fact contain a lot of teaching about the inter-connectedness of the believer and the world in which he or she lives.

The passage quoted at the beginning from Romans under-lines how the redemption of humankind is inseparably linked with God's purposes to restore the earth to its full creativity. The final redemption of all the sons and daughters of God will signal the healing of the earth itself. This is because, as the cursing of the earth was a consequence of Adam's sin (Genesis 3:17–19), so the full redemption of Adam's descendants will be the occasion to release the earth from its curse and restore it to its full splendour as the work of the divine creator who said when it was first made, 'It is good'.

However, because the ground has been cursed it does not mean that the creation itself has been condemned. Therefore we read that the heavens declare the glory of the Lord (Psalm 19:1; 89:5) and that they proclaim his righteousness (Psalm 50:6). The earth itself will sing to the Lord (Psalm 96:1,11), for everything in it belongs to the Lord (Psalm 24:1); conse-quently the glory of the Lord is still to be found in the earth he has created (Numbers 14:21). Indeed, as Jesus himself taught his disciples, God's will is to be done upon the earth in just the same way as it is being done in heaven (Matthew 6:10).

An example of a Christian spirituality which offers us a biblical response to the issues of the Lordship of Christ and the way he continues to speak through and with his creation, is the Celtic church. They saw God healing creation from the inside through Jesus who was, after all, the Lamb slain from the foundation of the world (Revelation 13:8). In other words, the healing agendas for the material creation and human creation were formulated and acted upon as one indivisible project. This is also the case when we glimpse through the visions of the Apostle John, the reuniting of a new heaven and earth with the new nation of God's redeemed people (Revel-ation 21:1–4). The Celts believed very much in seeing the invisible presence of God within his visible creation. According to David Adam, they did not see God in all his glory more than we do, but they were more aware of signs of his presence.[3]

These signs were written large in the creation itself. The nearness of God to and in his creation brought a strong sense that the heavenly powers were not far away, but surrounded everyone in both day and night. Consequently work and worship and wonder formed an interweaving pattern of growing awareness of the presence and power of God in every department of his creation. There are prayers for the milking of cows, for the lighting of fires, and for driving the flocks through the fields. It felt quite natural to invoke the heavenly powers, saints and angels throughout the day. The clouds brought to mind the presence of angels, the thunderstorm spoke of the wrestling with dark powers that the Christian constantly faced. Compare the words of the famous prayer attributed to St Patrick:

> I arise today
> Through the strength of Heaven:
> Light of the sun,
> Radiance of moon,
> Splendour of fire,
> Speed of lightning,
> Swiftness of wind,
> Depth of sea,
> Stability of earth,
> Firmness of rock.[4]

Many of the prayers and hymns of the Celtic people were in fact carefully collected by Alexander Carmichael who published them under the title of the *Carmina Gadelica*[5] and they illustrate this interweaving of God's voice in creation with prayers of intercession and blessing. Here is just one example:

> The love and affection of heaven be to you,
> The love and affection of saints be to you,
> The love and affection of the angels be to you,
> The love and affection of the sun be to you,
> The love and affection of the moon be to you,
> Each day and night of your lives,
> To keep you from haters,

To keep you from harmers,
To keep you from oppressors.[6]

By being more open to how God's creation speaks out the praises and the presence of its creator we become more focused on the immediacy and the wonder of Emmanuel, God with us. There is also the fact that we have a duty to work in harmony with God's creation and not to despise it nor treat it cheaply (Genesis 2:15). There are a number of times in Scripture when we are reminded that the sins committed by people do affect the very ground and space upon which they are committed. Consider, for example, the passage in Leviticus which says 'If you defile the land it will vomit you out as it vomited out the nations that were before you' (Leviticus 18:28). The context for this is that of conquest and the occupation of the promised land. The people of Israel are challenged to a life of obedience and holiness if they wish to retain occupation of the land and if they wish the land to prove a blessing to them and not a curse. The connection between human sinfulness and damage to the land is widened still further by Hosea, one of the eighth-century Old Testament prophets. The prophet describes how the nation had forgotten how to love and that the land was filled with lying, cursing and murder. He goes on to say that 'because of this the land mourns, and all the people who live in it waste away; the beasts of the field and the birds of the air and the fish of the sea are dying' (Hosea 4:1–3). The other side of this connectedness between humanity and the land are those descriptions in the Bible which speak of the creation being blessed when the people of God walk in the ways of God. We read that the desert and the parched land will be glad; the wilderness will rejoice and blossom (Isaiah 35: 1, 4–7).

We do need therefore to recover our ministry to the earth which has been given into our stewardship, as well as appreciate and be aware of creation's ability to present us with signs of the Creator's presence amongst us. For the latter I could do no better as a beginning than to recommend Brother Ramon's book *Heaven and Earth* which takes the form of a personal retreat programme focused upon hearing and seeing God in his creation.[7] Regarding our stewardships to the earth, I would like to look particularly at the area of healing and deliverance.

So often the sins committed in one particular place affect that place for the forseeable future. God challenged Cain with the blood of his murdered brother Abel, which was literally crying out from the very ground which had received it (Genesis 4:10–12). It is also interesting to note that the ground which Cain will work upon is similarly cursed for his sins as was Adam's. The writers to the Hebrews links this theme of land being able to retain and speak of what happened upon it with the way in which the death of Christ on Calvary still speaks today, but this time of much better things (Hebrews 12:24).

There are times, I am sure, when we need not only to repent of our sins towards God but also to ask God to heal his earth and remove from it the effects of our sins and to restore his creation in order to make it a blessing and not a curse to us. This linking of healing of the land and the forgiveness of sins is to be found in the classic challenge to national holiness in the reign of King Solomon. The exhortation to repentance is given in the context of the land being devoured by locusts, plague and drought: 'If my people who are called by my name, will humble themselves and pray and seek my face and turn from their wicked ways, then will I hear from heaven and will forgive their sin and will heal their land' (2 Chronicles 7:14). This was a challenge for the nation to become aware not only of their sins and the need for repentance and forgiveness, but also to see their ministry to bring healing to the land. This is not to advocate that every natural disaster or trouble is a consequence of our sins, but it is a reminder that our sins do affect not only personal relationships but also the earth itself. Therefore it is not as far fetched as it may sound for us to ask God to bring healing to the places we live in and the very ground upon which we tread when he sets us free from our sins.

Consider also how many encouragements there are to pray for the peace of Jerusalem, or literally to go around the city and speak peace to her walls (Psalm 122:6–9). This is an extra resource to those times when we are engaged in spiritual warfare. Part of the preparation for successful battle against the forces of darkness sometimes focuses upon discerning whether there are any demonic powers which have in some way gained a hold or influence over an area. This seems to be suggested by the revelation of the angel to Daniel, who said that as he had been praying there had been a spiritual battle in the heavens between the archangel Michael and a power described as the prince of the Persian kingdom (Daniel: 1–2, 12–14). There has been much recently written on this subject of 'territorial spirits',[8] but unfortunately not many have given much thought to the need to apply the ministry of forgiveness to the land. I think that there are times, far from seeking demonic strongholds without our communities, when we need to have a prayer march which seeks out the parts of our towns, cities and countryside for which we want to give God thanks and ask him to make them a focus on his blessing and joy. I was struck recently by a comment made by Gerald Coates, one of the organizers of the Marches for Jesus which have become a feature of church witness across the world. He said that it did not matter if nobody came out on the streets to listen to the witness of the marchers, the important thing was that the land and the city itself heard about the praises of Jesus.

I do not underestimate the fact of demonic warfare, but I do plead for the ministry of forgiveness to be applied to the land and the city so that they too can be healed. We need to seek the face of God and repent of the destructive effects we have had upon this earth. We need to ask the Lord to lift his curse from the ground upon which we have sinned so that his blessings can return to the earth and it can once again sing the praises and the glory of its creator.

> Lord have mercy on us,
> Come and heal our land,
> Cleanse with your fire,
> Heal with your touch,
> Humbly we bow and call upon you now,
> O Lord have mercy on us.
> O Lord have mercy on us.[9]

God bless the earth
And all living creatures
God bless the earth
With its rugged features
God bless the earth
Every town and city
God bless the earth
With all its industry
God bless the earth
Atmosphere and air
God bless the earth
Keep it in your care
God bless the earth
Protect the living soil
God bless the earth
May nothing despoil
God bless the earth
And its daily light
God bless the earth
Preserve it by your might.[10]

Appendix 1

An Exercise in Forgiveness

The following exercise is designed for use within any form of church service. It is an opportunity for a congregation to exercise its God-given calling to be both the body of Christ for others and also to fulfil its role as a holy and royal priesthood which offers spiritual sacrifices acceptable to God through Jesus Christ (1 Peter 2:5,9). It is also a reminder to us that the minister who announces the forgiveness of God for us following our confession is not there to replace our sharing in this calling but to represent and resource us so that we too fulfil our priestly calling. Finally let us remind ourselves that it is only God through Jesus Christ who forgives sins; this exercise is one way of enabling others to enter into this reality.

1 Before beginning a leader will explain the nature of the exercise and then invite the Holy Spirit to come down upon every heart open to God and show them any area in their lives into which they need to bring God's forgiveness and healing.

Take a little time to explain that the basic meaning of the word 'to forgive' means 'let go'. Here we have an opportunity, in the presence of God, to discover what we are holding against other people and come to the Lord Jesus and ask his help to 'let go' and go free in the power of the Holy Spirit. You may like to use the 'Jungle Doctor' story definition of forgiveness (see page 14).

The leader will also speak quite deliberately and slowly, and, where appropriate, leave short silences at various points in order to allow everyone to get fully involved in the exercise. Allow about 5–10 minutes for this exercise.

2   Find a partner with whom you wish to share this time of
    ministry and then either sit together or, better still, find a
    place in the church where you can stand together facing
    each other.

3   Decide between yourselves who is going to be the minister
    of forgiveness in the name and power of Jesus. Once this
    is done, the 'ministers' stand in front of their partners with
    both of their hands extended openly towards them whilst
    they pray silently. This is to remind you that our Lord Jesus
    opened wide his arms for you upon the cross and waits for
    you to come to him in need and he will hear and receive
    you.

4   Now will the one who is praying just wait upon God and
    silently ask the Lord to make you aware of any person or
    event or feeling which still causes you bitterness or hurt.
    When you are sure that you know what this is, then allow
    yourself to become aware of holding these memories or
    people or events in the palm of your right hand. Close your
    right hand into a fist and say silently to God:

    Lord these are the things that I have been holding in my
    heart. You see how I have refused to forgive in the past,
    but today I want to say I am sorry to you and set these
    people, these past moments, these hurting feelings, free
    from my unforgiving heart.

    Now take a few moments to name specifically before God
    the people you wish to forgive. You may even want to
    name yourself because you failed to do something and have
    caused someone a lot of pain and heartache as a result.
    Perhaps you want to say sorry to God because you have
    held bitter feelings against him because things have not
    worked as you had hoped and it has made you bitter against
    him.
    Please do not tell your partner what it is you are confess-

ing towards God, but feel free to tell them afterwards only if you want to and you think it will help.

5 Once you have named these people before God and asked for forgiveness, hand over what you have been holding in your closed fist into the open hand of your 'minister'. Literally place the whole lot into the open palm of your partner. This is your way of saying that you will no longer hold such unforgiveness towards others.

6 Now will all the 'ministers' close their hands over whatever sins have been placed in them and with as much confidence as possible raise this hand up towards heaven and throw the sins away at the feet of Jesus. Straight afterwards I want you to look at your partner (do not stare!), and, with eyes open, say their name to them and declare:

> (*Name of the person*), Jesus says that because you have confessed your sins he now forgives you and cleanses you from all unrighteousness. Therefore be healed and go free in the name of Jesus Christ.

7 Finally, will the person who has just been praying give you a minute or two to pray your own prayer saying that you thank God for his forgiveness and take it into your heart and will determine by the grace of God to walk in the newness of life which Jesus gives.

NB.   Allow some minutes for the possibility of further ministry and prayer resulting from this. The leader might like to say something to this effect. Often some people want to share something that has come out of this work and then be prayed over again. When you feel that most people have completed this work then ask everyone to return to their seats as you are about to continue. However, there will be opportunity for further counsel at the end of the service should people like to make use of this.

Appendix 2

Forgiveness is Healing

The following is a detailed prayer of forgiveness which can be used as part of a penitential service for personal healing or for the healing and renewal of the Church. It can also be used for special occasions such as a watch-night service in preparation for the new year, or on Easter Saturday evening as the church prepares to come out of the darkness of the grave into the brilliance of the resurrection morning of new life in the Holy Spirit. The minister or leader is to read the whole prayer quite steadily and in small portions so that the congregation may repeat it after him. He or she is to remind the congregation that whilst every issue might not be relevant to them as individuals they might well be relevant for the fellowship as a whole.

As we share in this prayer, let the Holy Spirit move freely and guide your hearts and minds to persons or groups or moments in your life that you need to forgive:

Lord Jesus Christ, I ask today to forgive everyone in my life. Please give me the grace of your Holy Spirit to open my heart to every person or moment you wish me to forgive. Find a way through my pain or hard heart so that I might free others from my unforgiveness and see your healing power in my life, in others and in my church. This I ask in the name of the Lord Jesus Christ, Amen.

Lord, I forgive MYSELF for my sins, faults and failings. For all that is truly bad, I do forgive myself. For any delvings into the occult, ouija boards, horoscopes, seances, fortune telling, lucky charms. For taking your name in vain; for not worshipping you. For hurting my parents; for getting drunk; for taking drugs; for sins against my purity; for adultery; for abortion; for stealing; for lying. I am truly forgiving myself today. Thank you Lord for your grace at this moment.

I truly forgive my MOTHER. I forgive her for all the times she hurt me, she resented me, she was angry with me, and for all the times she punished me. I forgive her for all the times she preferred my brothers and sisters to me. I forgive her for the times she told me I was dumb, ugly, stupid, the worst of the children or that I cost the family a lot of money. For the times she told me that I was unwanted, an accident, a mistake or not what she expected; I forgive her.

I forgive my FATHER. I forgive him for any non-support, any lack of love, affection or attention. I forgive him for any lack of time, for not giving me his companionship, for his drinking or arguing and fighting with my mother or the other children. For his severe punishments, for desertion, for being away from home, for divorcing my mother or for any running around; I do forgive him.

Lord, I extend forgiveness to my SISTERS AND BROTHERS. I forgive those who rejected me, lied about me, hated me, resented me, competed for my parents' love, those who hurt me, who physically harmed me. For those who were too severe on me, punished me or made my life unpleasant in any way, I do forgive them.

Lord, I do forgive my SPOUSE for lack of love, affection, consideration, support, attention, communication, for fault, failings, weaknesses and those other acts or words that hurt or disturb me.

Jesus, I forgive my CHILDREN for their lack of respect, obedience, love, attention, support, warmth, understanding;

their bad habits, falling away from following you; any bad actions which disturb me.

My God, I forgive my SON/DAUGHTER-IN-LAW and other relatives by marriage, who treat my child with a lack of love. For all their words, thoughts, actions, or omissions which injure and cause pain: I forgive them.

Please help me to forgive my RELATIVES, my grandmother and grandfather who may have interfered in our family, been possessive of my parents, who may have caused confusion or turned one parent against another.

Jesus, help me to forgive my CO-WORKERS who are dis-agreeable or make life miserable for me. For those who push their work off on to me, gossip about me, won't co-operate with me, try to take my job; I do forgive them.

I now forgive my MINISTER, CHURCH, CONGRE-GATION for all their lack of support, pettiness, lack of friendliness, for not affirming me as they should; for not providing me with inspiration; for not using me in a proper way; for not inviting me to have a share in the work of ministry; for any hurt they have inflicted; I do forgive them today.

Lord, I forgive all professional people who have hurt me in any way: doctors, nurses, lawyers, policemen, social workers. For anything they did to me; I do forgive them today.

Lord, I forgive my EMPLOYER for not paying me enough money, for not appreciating my work, for being unkind and unreasonable to me, for being angry or unfriendly, for not promoting me and for not complimenting me on my work; I do forgive them today.

Lord, I forgive my SCHOOL TEACHERS and other INSTRUCTORS, of the past as well as the present. For those who punished me, humiliated me, treated me unjustly, made fun of me, called me dumb or stupid, made me stay after school.

Lord, I forgive my FRIENDS who have let me down, lost contact with me; do not support me, were not available when I needed help, borrowed money and did not return it, gossiped about me; I do forgive them all dear Lord.

Lord Jesus, I especially pray for the grace of forgiveness for that ONE PERSON in life who has hurt me the most. I ask to forgive anyone whom I consider my greatest enemy, the one who is the hardest to forgive, or the one whom I said I will never forgive.

Pour out your Holy Spirit upon me Lord Jesus and help me to let go of all that I hold against these people and set me free to live a new life free from evil. I give you thanks that you always hear and answer my prayer. So now I praise God that he is helping me to forgive. Please reach out to all those people I have mentioned who need your help and healing and give them the touch of your healing presence. All these things I ask for and give you thanks through the name of our Lord Jesus Christ. Amen.

(This form of prayer is adapted from that of the same name by Father Robert DeGrandis, a leader in Charismatic Renewal in the Roman Catholic Church in the United States.)

Appendix 3

A Service for a Christian Day of Atonement

Preparation

Before holding one of these services the leader(s) of the church needs first to recognize the need for healing the relationships within the fellowship of the church. When such breakdowns in relationship have been allowed to fester or remain unattended for many generations, they become a foothold for the Devil and evil. When this happens the church is already seriously weakened in its spiritual warfare, and its witness to the gospel of Jesus Christ is greatly diminished. The leader(s) should also give some teaching on the connection between the need to forgive and the power to be released from the effects of evil. Consequently the congregation should be asked to prepare their hearts for such a service and come with the intention specifically to own any area in their shared, or even personal, lives where they need to be forgiven or to offer forgiveness in the power of Jesus Christ. It should also be stressed that the way the ministry of forgiveness is offered in the service can be either privately, in the form of writing down the names of people or times you wish to forgive and placing these on the Lord's table during some form of offertory; or it can be done publicly by giving people an opportunity during an extended Peace to share the Peace, in particular with those with whom they wish to be reconciled.

This service can take the form of Communion or it can be a fairly free form of service. The liturgy below can be used, or another if required. The various hymns and readings are a suggestion only and can also be changed if necessary.

Opening Sentences

LEADER Behold how good and pleasant it is when we live together in unity.

ALL It is like precious oil poured on the head.

LEADER Here is the place where God will command his blessings for us, even life for evermore.

ALL Amen!

Collect/Prayer of Invocation

ALL O God our Father, we praise you that you have made your Son Jesus Christ, Lord of our Church. Come now by your Holy Spirit and set our hearts on fire with love for you and one another. Renew your church to be a powerful witness in this land as we know the healing of your forgiveness amongst us, through Jesus Christ our Lord. Amen.

Hymn

Be thou my vision (*Mission Praise 1*, No. 17)
There is a Redeemer (*Mission Praise 2*, No. 590)
Praise my Soul the King of Heaven (*Cry Hosanna*, No. 18)

Readings

Psalm 15; 24; 32; 85

Silence to meditate upon the word.

OT
  Leviticus 16
  Exekiel 45: 17–20
  Isaiah 55; 64

Song
  Search me O God (*Mission Praise 1*, No. 200)
  Father I Place (*Mission Praise 1*, No. 45)
  Soften my Heart, by Graham Kendrick (Make Way Music 1988)

NT
  Matthew 18: 21–35
  Luke 15: 8–32
  2 Corinthians 2:5–11

Homily/Sermon

On the theme of forgiveness and healing. Conclude with an opportunity for everyone to dedicate afresh their lives to God. This can be through silent prayer or by way of singing one of the following suggested songs:

Adoramus te Domine (We adore you O God/Taizé) – sung gently for a few minutes as a way of offering one's life to God.
Here I am wholly available (*Mission Praise 2*, No. 393)
Make me a channel (*Mission Praise 1*, No. 153)
O breath of life come sweeping through us (*Mission Praise 1*, No. 164)
Soften my heart (Shine, Jesus shine)
Take my life (*Mission Praise 1*, No. 217)

Affirmation

The Nicene Creed
or
We Believe, by Graham Kendrick

Penitence

LEADER Our Lord Jesus Christ calls us to be a people who know how to forgive one another. Let us then come humbly and boldly into his light so that we may first receive forgiveness for our sins and then offer this freedom to those who have hurt us in some way

ALL   Father eternal, giver of light and grace, we have sinned against you and against others in what we have thought, in what we have said and done, through ignorance, through weakness, through our own deliberate fault.

We have wounded your love,
and marred your image in us.
We are sorry and ashamed,
and repent of our sins.
For the sake of your Son, Jesus Christ, who died for us, forgive us all that is past; and lead us out from darkness to walk as the children of light. Amen.
(*Slightly adapted from ASB*)

LEADER Almighty God forgive you and cleanse you from all unrighteousness in the name of our Lord Jesus Christ and through the power of his Holy Spirit coming upon you now. So rejoice and give God thanks for his gift of cleansing and release.

Offering Forgiveness to Others

LEADER Having received God's forgiveness for ourselves, we can now be open to God to show us who it is that he requires us to forgive. Let us be still before the Lord and allow him to make us aware of who we need to forgive.

A time of silence whilst people write down the names of those they want to free from their unforgiving attitude. (You can also use the form in Appendix 1.) When there has been sufficient time, explain to people that they are to bring their pieces of paper (which will not be read) and place them in a suitable basket which is placed either on the altar or on a table at the front of the church. There can be some gentle singing whilst time is given for people to come forward.

LEADER (*Hold up all the pieces of paper to God.*) Dear Lord, we ask you to look upon the lives of all those written here. You know fully how their lives and actions have touched us and hurt us. But today we turn to you and say that through the grace of God given to us, we let go of holding anything against them and choose to forgive them and free them from our unforgiveness. Send out your Holy Spirit upon us and them and bring us all your healing power to make us whole, through Jesus Christ our Lord.

ALL   Amen!

The Peace

LEADER Let us now share Christ's powerful peace with one another to show that he has made us one family and one fellowship. The peace of the Lord be always with you.

ALL   And also with you.

Hymn

Come Holy Ghost our souls inspire (*Mission Praise 1*, No. 36)
God forgave my sin (*Mission Praise 1*, No. 60)
Restore O Lord (*Mission Praise 1*, No. 196)
Rejoice! Rejoice! (*Mission Praise 2*, No. 543)

Prayers of Cleansing and Battle

LEADER Now that the Lord has renewed our unity in the Holy Spirit, it is time to ask him to deliver us from anything that has been said and done in the life of this church which has grieved his Holy Spirit.

Here each church must be free to address its own history and any particular issues which are known to have been damaging or compromising to the church's witness and life. Here we must be careful not to focus on any one group or individual within the life of the church but encourage everyone to own as theirs the sins of the past. A particular way of doing this is to identify prominent foci for ministry in the church such as

- the pulpit
- the communion table or rail
- the choir stalls
- the baptismal font
- the vestry
- the wardens' seats

– the minister's seat

Over each, with the laying on of hands by a representative group of the church, pray a prayer along the lines of the following:

Heavenly Lord, we ask you now in the power and authority of Jesus Christ, that you forgive anything said or done in this place which has grieved your Spirit and provided Satan with a foothold in the life of our church. In the name of Jesus we command that all ties to ungodliness be broken, the powers of darkness be destroyed and the cleansing power of the blood of Jesus restore this to be a place of blessing and healing, through Jesus Christ our Lord. Amen.

Finally, let there be a few minutes whereby the entire congregation is given an opportunity to lay hands on their leaders and pray for God's healing, encouragement and anointing upon their ministry. That they be renewed in the power of the Holy Spirit.

Hymn

The battle belongs to the Lord (*Song Gifts*, 84)
Shine, Jesus shine (Thankyou Music 1987)
Light has dawned (*Songs of Fellowship* 2)
For this purpose (*Mission Praise 2*, No. 358)
Lord have mercy on us (*Mission Praise 2, No. 481*)

Prayer of Dismissal
or
Holy Communion/Breaking of Bread

Final hymn

Tell out my soul (*Mission Praise 1*, No. 215)
O for a thousand tongues to sing (*Mission Praise 1*, No. 168)
The king is amongst us (*Mission Praise 1*, No. 222)
Jesus put this song into my heart (*Mission Praise 1*, No. 457)

Notes

INTRODUCTION

1. David Runcorn, *Touch Wood* (Darton, Longman & Todd 1992), p. 39.
2. Corrie Ten Boom, *Tramp for the Lord* (Hodder & Stoughton 1975), pp. 56–7.
3. Jim Cotter, *Prayer at Night* (Cairns Publications 1988), p. 79.
4. 'Healing Harvest' quoted in Matthew and Dennis Linn, *Healing Life's Hurts* (Paulist Press 1978), p. ix.

1   FORGIVENESS IN ACTION

1. Lewis Smedes, *Forgive and Forget* (Triangle 1988), p. ix.
2. James G. Emerson, *The Dynamics of Forgiveness* (George Allen & Unwin 1965), p. 55.
3. *Letter to Barnabas, The Apostolic Fathers*, tr. F. Glimm, J. Marique and G. Walsh, *The Fathers of the Church*, Vol. 4 (Cima Publishing Company Inc. 1947), p. 200.
4. Rudolph Bultmann, 'Forgiveness', *Theological Dictionary of the New Testament*, ed. Gerhard Kittel and Gerhard Friedrich; abridged in one volume by Geoffrey W. Bromiley (Eerdmans 1990), p. 88.
5. cf. Warren Wiersbe, *The Bible Exposition Commentary*, Vol. 1 (Victor Books 1989), p. 275; J. Norval Geldenhuys, *Commentary on the Gospel of Luke* (Marshall, Morgan and Scott 1971), p. 608.

6. Emil Brunner, *The Mediator* (Lutterworth Press 1952), p. 423.

7. F. B. Meyer, *Our Daily Walk* (Grand Rapids, Zondervan, 1951), p. 142.

8. Lewis Smedes, op. cit., p. xii.

9. James G. Emerson, op. cit., p. 75.

10. David Runcorn, *Touch Wood*, (Darton, Longman & Todd 1992), p. 64.

11. Jim Graham, *Forgiveness* (Scripture Union 1991), p. 15.

12. Francis Brown, S. R. Driver and Charles A. Briggs (eds.), *Hebrew and English Lexicon of the Old Testament* (Clarendon Press 1977), p. 497.

13. William Gesenius, *Hebrew and Chaldee Lexicon*, tr. S. P. Tregellis (Eerdmans 1949), p. 588.

14. The three remaining words are *apoluo*, which means to 'loose away'; *aphesis*, which means to 'let go'; and *charizomai*, which means to 'be gracious to'. Vincent Taylor says that this latter term brings with it the thought of setting aside, through love, the barriers in the way of fellowship (Vincent Taylor, *Forgiveness and Reconciliation* (Macmillan and Co 1960), p. 6).

15. James Denney, quoted in H. R. Mackintosh, *The Christian Experience of Forgiveness* (Nisbet 1944), p. 187.

16. John Owen, *The Forgiveness of Sin* (Grand Rapids, Baker Book House, 1977), pp. 115–17.

17. David Runcorn, op. cit., p. 40.

2 THE POWER TO FORGIVE

1. Simon Barrington-Ward, 'A New Belonging', *CMS Newsletter*, July 1979.

2. Jim Graham, *Forgiveness* (Scripture Union 1991), p. 18.

3. cf. for example, Daniel 9:5, 8, 11, 15; Jeremiah 3:25; Ezra 10:13. Daniel is in fact listed in Ezekiel 14:14, 20 as one of the three outstanding righteous men of his era.

4. Emil Brunner, *The Mediator* (Lutterworth Press 1952), p. 480.

5. Jim Graham, op. cit., p. 24.
6. Rita Bennett, *Inner Wholeness through the Lord's Prayer* (Kingsway 1991), p. 109.
7. John Calvin, *Institutes of Christian Religion*, ed. John T. McNeill (The Westminster Press, Library of Christian Classics, 1960), Vol. XX, IV, p. 22.
8. Compare such verses as Luke 9:1–6 (sending out of the twelve); Luke 10:1–24 (sending out of the seventy or seventy-two; note the similarity of proclamation, ministry and tactic); Matthew 28: 18–20 (the great commission). Compare also the reference in 1 Peter 2:9 which speaks of the royal priesthood of all believers.
9. If you would like to know more about accreditation and training for Christian counsellors, you might like to contact the Association of Christian Counsellors, King's House, 175 Wokingham Road, Reading, Berkshire, RG6 1LU.
10. Janet Street-Porter, quoted in Lord Longford, *Forgiveness of Man by Man* (Buchebroc Press 1989), p. 40.
11. C. S. Lewis, *Fern-Seeds and Elephants*, ed. W. Hooper (Collins, Fount paperbacks, 1975), p. 40.
12. David Runcorn, *Touch Wood* (Darton, Longman & Todd 1992), p. 46.
13. John White, *Changing on the Inside* (Eagle 1991), pp. 130–3.
14. James G. Emerson, *The Dynamics of Forgiveness* (George Allen & Unwin 1965), p. 73.

3 FORGIVENESS AND SALVATION

1. H. R. Mackintosh, *The Christian Experience of Forgiveness* (Nisbet and Co. Ltd 1944), p. 87.
2. David Runcorn, *Touch Wood* (Darton, Longman & Todd 1992), p. 64.
3. W. Foerster in *Theological Dictionary of the New Testament*, eds. G. Kittel and G. Friedrich (Eerdmans 1971), Vol. 7, p. 900.

4. Dietrich Bonhoeffer, *The Cost of Discipleship*, SCM 1964.
5. Morris Maddocks, *The Christian Healing Ministry* (SPCK 1985), p. 12.
6. John Owen, *The Forgiveness of Sin* (Baker Book House 1977), p. 62.
7. Emil Brunner, *The Mediator* (Lutterworth Press 1952), p. 449.
8. H. R. Mackintosh, op. cit., p. 25.
9. John Owen, op. cit., p. 71.
10. Rita Bennett, *Inner Wholeness Through the Lord's Prayer* (Kingsway 1991), p. 107.
11. For further connections between repentance and forgiveness, compare Mark 4:12, Acts 2:38; 5:31; 8:22; 26:18. If you wish to study this connection in more detail then read Vincent Taylor, *Forgiveness and Reconciliation* (Macmillan & Company 1960), pp. 7–9; he lists thirty more references to repentance where the idea of forgiveness is lying in the background.
12. Arthur B. L. Karney, *The Father and his Sons* (SPCK 1937), pp. 23,29.
13. Morris Maddocks, op. cit., p. 12.
14. John White, *Changing on the Inside* (Eagle 1991), p. 39.
15. C. S. Lewis, *Mere Christianity* (Fontana 1950), p. 114.
16. Basilea Schlink, *Repentance: The Joy-filled Life*, Oliphants 1969.
17. Robin Green, *A Step too Far* (Darton, Longman & Todd 1990), p. 26.
18. ibid., p. 46.
19. Emil Brunner, op. cit. Read the third section, chapters 15–21.
20. Robin Green, op. cit., p. 51.
21. Compare Titus 3:5–7; also Ephesians 5:27; Philippians 1:10, 15; 1 Thessalonians 3:15, 23, speak of the goal of blamelessness to which each Christian is called. John 3:1–3 also speaks of the ultimate goal of our Christ-likeness.
22. Martin H. Padovani, *Healing Wounded Emotions* (Twenty-Third Publications 1987), p.44.

23. Article on Forgiveness in *The Interpreter's Dictionary of the Bible*, ed. George A Buttrick (Abingdon Press 1962), Vol. 2, p. 317.
24. John Calvin, *Institutes*, ed. John T. McNeill (The Westminster Press, Library of Christian Classics, 1960), Vol. XX, IV, p. 22.
25. Mick Ray, 'I Get So Excited, Lord' (Thankyou Music, PO Box 75, Eastbourne, BN23 6NW).
26. Donald W. Shriver Jr, *Forgiveness and Politics: The Case of the American Black Civil Rights Movement* (New World Publications 1987), p. 8.
27. Henri Nouwen, *In the House of the Lord* (Darton, Longman & Todd 1986), p. 41.

4 FORGIVENESS AND HEALING THE FELLOWSHIP

1. Jenny Cook, *Love and Acceptance and Forgiveness* (Regal Books 1984), pp. 90–1.
2. A. R. George, *Communion with God in the New Testament* (Inter Varsity Press 1953), p. 133, quoted in *The Illustrated Bible Dictionary*, ed. J. D. Douglas (Inter Varsity Press 1980), p. 307. Words in brackets mine.
3. For a fuller account of the story you can read *Lord of the Years* by Geraint Fielder (Inter Varsity Press 1989), pp. 227–9. This is a book about the first sixty years of the Inter-Varsity Fellowship and the Union of College Christian Fellowships.
4. There are in fact approximately 145 references to fellowship offerings in the Old Testament.
5. J. I. Durham, quoted in *The New International Dictionary of New Testament Theology* (Paternoster 1976), Vol. 2, p. 778.
6. Hans Küng, quoted in Jim Graham, *Forgiveness* (Scripture Union 1991), p. 106.
7. M. Scott Peck, *The Road Less Travelled* (Simon and Schuster 1978), p. 45.

8. cf. also John 15:12, 17; 1 John 3:23, 4:21; 2 John 5, 6 for further examples of the command to love.

9. Other images of the essential unity in relationship for the Church are the vine and the branches (John 15:1–5), the shepherd and the sheep (John 10:11; Hebrews 13:20; 1 Peter 2:9; Revelation 1:6; 5:10; 20:6).

10. J. I. Packer, *Keep in Step with the Spirit* (Inter Varsity Press 1984), pp. 101–2.

11. John White, *Changing on the Inside* (Eagle 1991), p. 94.

12. For a fuller list of commands to separate from and put out of the church those who refuse the disciplines of the church, look at pp. 714–16 in H. L. Wilmington, *Guide to the Bible*, Tyndale House 1986.

13. ibid., p. 715.

14. Francis Brown, S. R. Driver and Charles A. Briggs (eds.), *Hebrew and English Lexicon of the Old Testament* (Clarendon Press 1977), p. 497.

15. *Second Letter of Clement, The Apostolic Fathers*, tr., F. Glimm, J. Marique and G. Walsh, *The Fathers of the Church*, Vol. 1 (Cima Publishing Company Inc. 1947), p. 74.

16. Martin Luther, quoted in William Telfer, *The Forgiveness of Sins* (SCM 1959), p. 109.

5 FORGIVENESS AND PERSONAL HEALING

1. Lawrence O. Richards, *Expository Dictionary of Bible Words* (Marshall Pickering 1988), pp. 158–9.

2. Donald Coggan, *Convictions* (Hodder & Stoughton 1975), p. 272.

3. cf. Mark 2:9; Luke 9:2; 10:5–9.

4. cf. also Psalm 6:7; 16:9; 32:3–5; 40:12.

5. John Phillips, *Exploring the Psalms*, Vol. 1 (Loizeaux Brothers 1987), p. 287. C. F. Keil and F. Delitzsch, *Commentary on the Old Testament*, Vol. 5, *The Psalms* (1989), p. 21.

6. Charles Haddon Spurgeon, *Treasury of David*, Vol. 2 (Marshall Brothers 1870) p. 227.

7. Read the whole of the article entitled 'Somatisers and Healing' in *The Independent*, 3 September 1991. There are useful sections in M. Scott Peck's *People of the Lie* (Touchstone Books 1985) where he speaks of the physical and mental damage due to the presence of evil (pp. 120f), and chapter 5 of David Benner's *Psychotherapy and the Spiritual Quest* (Hodder & Stoughton 1988) which deals with the cumulative effects of inner distress upon the whole person.

8. Matthew and Dennis Linn, *Healing Life's Hurts* (Paulist Press 1978), p. 36.

9. ibid.

10. *The Independent*, 3 September 1991.

11. ibid.

12. Charles Williams, *The Forgiveness of Sins* (Geoffrey Bles 1942), p. 56.

13. Rita Bennett, *Inner Wholeness through the Lord's Prayer* (Kingsway 1991), p. 119.

14. For a fuller version of this story you might like to read my book, *Healing Dreams* (SPCK 1987), pp. 1–6.

15. David Seamands, *Healing the Memories* (Victor Books 1986), p. 76.

16. There are two excellent books which teach the value of learned listening skills; they are Anne Long, *Listening* (Daybreak 1990), and Michael Mitton, *The Wisdom to Listen* (Grove Books 1991). You might also like to consider going on one of the varied listening courses offered by the Acorn Christian Healing Trust. Further information about these courses may be obtained from The Director, Whitehill Chase, High Street, Borden, Hants, GU35 0AP.

17. Teresa of Avila, *The Way of Perfection* Vol. 2, tr. E. Allison Peers (Sheed and Ward 1950), pp. 159–60.

18. Robert Bly, *Iron John* (Element Books 1990), p. 38.

19. Paul Tillich, *The Eternal Now* (Scribner 1963), quoted in Matthew and Dennis Linn, op. cit., p. 93.

20. Matthew and Dennis Linn, op. cit., p. 115.
21. See John 18:18; 21:9.
22. Thayer's *Greek–English Lexicon of the New Testament* (Associated Publishers 1972), p. 514.
23. Derek Prince, *Blessing or Curse?* (Word Books 1990), p. 109.

6 FORGIVENESS AND HEALING OF MEMORIES

1. Selwyn Hughes, *The Christian Counsellor*, Vol. 3 No. 3, p. 10.
2. David Seamands, ibid., p. 12.
3. There are approximately 250 references to the subject of remembering the Bible, 16 of which occur in the book of Deuteronomy. In the main they refer to the fact of God's continuing rememberance of his creation as opposed to mankind's failure to remember the covenants and calling of God upon him. At the heart of the Christian celebration of the Holy Communion or Lord's Supper is the injunction to remember Jesus and how what he has done at the cross will result in his return. cf. 1 Corinthians 11:25 and 2 Timothy 2:8.
4. John White, *Changing on the Inside* (Eagle 1991), p. 50.
5. Agnes Sanford, quoted in Leanne Payne *Restoring the Christian Soul* (Kingsway 1992), p. 68.
6. David Benner, *Healing Emotional Wounds* (Baker Book House 1990), pp. 18–19.
7. Derek Prince, *Blessing or Curse?* (Ward Books 1990), pp. 108–9.
8. ibid., pp. 97–100.
9. cf. Leanne Payne, op. cit., p. 75f. where she speaks of ancestral memories acting like imprints upon later generations. You may also like to read Dr Frank Lake's book *Tight Corners in Pastoral Care* (Darton, Longman & Todd 1981) where he refers to the unborn baby picking up some of the stresses of its mother and living them out in later life. There is also the biblical picture of Daniel and Ezra

praying to God for the results of their fathers' sins to be removed from the captive exiles so that they may be returned to their homeland and establish a people of Israel once again (Ezekiel 9:5–15; Daniel 9:4–19).

10. Robert Bly, *Iron John* (Element Books 1990), p. 147.
11. Sigmund Freud, quoted in Benner, op. cit., p. 93.
12. Elizabeth Kübler Ross, *Questions and Answers on Death and Dying* (Macmillan 1974), p. 31.
13. Dave Carder, quoted in *Secrets of Your Family Tree* by Dave Carder, Earl Henslen, John Townsend, Henry Cloud and Alice Braward (Moody Press 1991), p. 77.
14. Joseph Sica, *Marriage and Family Living*, August 1983, pp. 18–21.
15. Claudia Back, quoted in *Secrets of your Family Tree*, p. 71.
16. Dave Carder, op. cit., p. 83.
17. Some useful books have been written about the triggering of such early memories. You might like to read Arthur Janov, *Primal Scream* (Sphere 1973); Ruth Carter Stapleton, *The Experience of Inner Healing* (Hodder & Stoughton 1978); Michael Mitton and Russ Parker, *Requiem Healing* (Daybreak 1991).
18. For a more in-depth treatment of the subject of working with dreams see my books *Healing Dreams* (SPCK 1987); *Dreams and Spirituality* (Grove Books 1985); and the double cassette entitled, *Praying with Dreams* (Eagle 1992) which is a workshop approach to the subject and contains a live dream counselling process.
19. David Benner, op. cit., p. 63.
20. Dave Carder, op. cit., pp. 245–6.
21. Rita Bennett, *Inner Wholeness through the Lord's Prayer* (Kingsway 1991), p. 118.
22. Lewis Smedes, *Forgive and Forget* (Triangle 1988), p. 39.
23. Derek Prince, op. cit., p. 70.
24. A fuller explanation of this ministry is to be found in Michael Mitton and Russ Parker, op. cit.
25. Leanne Payne, op. cit., p. 90.
26. David Benner, op. cit., p. 44.

27. Matthew and Dennis Linn, *Healing Life's Hurts* (Paulist Press 1978), pp. 115–16.
28. William Blake, 'A Poison Tree', quoted in Myra Chave-Jones, *Living with Anger* (Triangle 1992), p. 98.

7 DELIVERANCE AND FORGIVENESS

1. Warren Wiersbe, *The Bible Exposition Commentary* (Victor Books 1989), p. 635.
2. The following is a selection of a number of useful books which explore spiritual warfare in a more in-depth manner: Graham Twelftree, *Christ Triumphant*, Hodder & Stoughton 1980; Michael Perry (ed.), *Deliverance*, SPCK 1987; John Richards, *But Deliver us from Evil*, Darton, Longman & Todd 1974; Russ Parker, *The Occult-Deliverance from Evil*, Inter Varsity Press 1989; Peter Horrobin, *Healing Through Deliverance*, Sovereign World 1991; C. Fred Dickason, *Demon Possession and the Christian*, Crossway 1990; Leon Suenens, *Renewal and the Powers of Darkness* Darton, Longman & Todd 1983.
3. John Richards, op. cit., p. 121.
4. C. Fred Dickason, op. cit., p. 62.
5. Lawrence O. Richards, *Expository Dictionary of Bible Words* (Marshall Pickering 1988), p. 62.
6. Thomas Brooks, *Precious Remedies Against Satan's Devices* (Banner of Truth Trust 1990), p. 56.
7. ibid., p. 57.
8. Peter Lombard, quoted in Bernhard Preschmann, *Penance and Anointing of the Sick* (Palm Tree Publishers 1964), p. 160.
9. Leon Suenens, op. cit., p. 26.
10. Lawrence O. Richards, op. cit., p. 283.
11. Mark I. Bubeck, *The Adversary* (Moody 1975), p. 34.
12. John Stott, *God's New Society*, The Bible Speaks Today Series, (Inter Varsity Press 1982), pp. 267–75.
13. Martyn Lloyd Jones, *Christian Warfare* (Banner of Truth Trust 1976), p. 192.

14. For a list of indicators of possible demonic influence, see my book, *The Occult*, pp. 22–25, 123–6.

15. Michael Harper, *Spiritual Warfare* (Hodder & Stoughton 1970), p. 108.

16. Suenens, op. cit., p. 31 (words in brackets mine).

17. A fuller examination of this aspect of how demonic spirits gain some form of hold on our lives is found in my book, *The Occult*, pp. 97–107.

18. William Gurnall, *The Christian in Complete Armour*, Vol. 2, abridged by Ruthanne Gurlock, Kay King, Karen Sloan and Candy Coan (Banner of Truth Trust 1988), p. 160.

19. Binding and loosing is also used in connection with building and nurturing the growth of the fellowship and protecting it from people who would disrupt its life. This is certainly the context in Matthew 16:19 and 18:18 and is supported by the weight of early church teaching.

20. Leanne Payne, *Restoring the Christian Soul* (Kingsway 1992), p. 92.

8 HEALING THE LAND THROUGH FORGIVENESS

1. The name 'Gaia' was suggested by the author William Golding to James Lovelock, an atmosphere scientist and inventor and member of the Royal Society, for his scientific concept of the living earth which he had called the biocybernetic universal system tendency/homeostasis.

2. Loren Wilkinson, in an article entitled 'How Christian is the Green Agenda?', *Christianity Today*, 11 January 1993, p. 16.

3. David Adam, *The Eye of the Eagle* (Triangle 1991), p. 7.

4. 'The Deer's Cry', 'The Hymn of St Patrick', from Kuno Meyer's *Selection from Ancient Irish Poetry* (Constable 1928), quoted in David Adam, *The Cry of the Deer* (Triangle 1991), pp. 3–4.

5. Alexander Carmichael *Carmina Gadelica*, Floris Books, 1992, abridged version.

6. ibid., Vol. 3, p. 209.

7. Brother Ramon, *Heaven and Earth*, Marshall Pickering 1991.
8. Example of such books on territorial warfare are: C. Peter Wagner, *Territorial Spirits*, Sovereign World 1991; John Dawson, *Taking our cities for God*, Word 1989; and Charles H. Kraft, *Defeating Dark Angels*, Servant Publications 1992.
9. Graham Kendrick, 'Lord Have Mercy On Us' (Thankyou Music, PO Box 75, Eastbourne, BN23 6NW).
10. David Adam, *Power Lines* (Triangle 1992), p. 39.